When the Smoke Clears:

A Phoenix Rises

By

Tenita C. Johnson

Published by
So It Is Written
Rochester Hills, MI
SoItIsWritten.net

Published by So It Is Written
Rochester Hills, MI
SoItIsWritten.net

When the Smoke Clears: A Phoenix Rises
Copyright ©2014 by Tenita C. Johnson

All rights reserved. No part of this book may be reproduced or transmitted in any form by any means without written permission of the publisher.

ISBN-13: 978-0-9904246-0-4
LCCN: 2014909258

Unless otherwise noted, all Scriptures are derived from the New Living Translation Bible.

Cover design by Jesse Cole
Author photograph by I See U Photography
Edited by Marcus Cylar of Cylar Consulting
Interior design by PenOfTheWriter.com

Printed in the USA

Dedication

I dedicate this book to the broken, the depressed, the oppressed, the cast down and the cast out.

I dedicate this book to my husband, my sole source of encouragement when everyone else walks away, Mr. Jermaine L. Johnson.

To my son, Jermaine Johnson II, thank you for reminding me that I shouldn't worry about things that haven't happened yet.

To Mrs. Izzie Lee Carson, no matter what fires I encountered in life, you always reminded me that it's alright—even when it wasn't. Thank you for your unconditional love and godly wisdom. You will truly be missed!

Lastly, but most importantly, I dedicate this book to God—my peace in the midst of the storms, my provider in times of lack and the Master of healing the broken.

Foreword

Some people will read this book because they are inquisitive and want to get the lowdown on the author's life. No doubt, they will find something of intrigue. If there was nothing in it about the smoke, the book would not be true to its title. Indeed, she did find herself seemingly beyond the reach of God at times. Clearly though, she is devoted to that same God who had the fondest thoughts of her, even before He formed her in her mother's womb—a single mother who, in fact, raised her to be self-sufficient and live her life without looking for scapegoats if she failed.

When the Smoke Clears is not a malicious exposé or carnal tell-all, although it does chronicle her life and reveal sensitive information. More importantly, though, it talks about the smoke clearing; and then the real purpose becomes obvious: the author wants to see other people emerge and come to the good future that truly exists for them. This book has no clichéd answers. Because she speaks from experience, not theory, her advice is qualified and her appeals to readers, who are still in the smoke, are passionate. Because as much as this book talks about the smoke, it is really about the smoke clearing and the phoenix arising from the fire.

Bishop John Fonzer

Table of Contents

Kudos! 11
Death Before Life 13
A Long Way from the Proverbs 31 Woman 23
It's Not All About You 37
The Void 51
When My Definition Changed 59
Defining the Madness 69
Built God-Tough 77
The Day of Rebirth 87
The Prayer of the Heart 97
Intentionally Specific 103
When the Smoke Clears 109
About Tenita C. Johnson 115
About So It Is Written 116

Kudos!

Giving all honor and glory to God, who is the head of my life, I thank you, Heavenly Father, for using me as the vessel to speak to your people in the midst of these despairing times. Like the saying goes, if I had 10,000 tongues, I couldn't praise you enough for all you have done in my life. God, I thank you for your mercy, your grace, your peace in the midst of my mess. Who wouldn't serve a God like this? Your rewards are priceless and limitless. You always exceeded my expectations, blessed me when I didn't deserve it, and had plans for me that even I myself couldn't fathom. I pray this book touches everyone you planned for this book to touch, reaches them right at the point of their need, and ministers to them like only your Spirit can. Now and forevermore, you are God and God alone. I will forever praise and worship you.

I would also like to thank my mother for pushing me to my limits when I thought she was being very, very strict. I thank my grandmother for helping raise me and steer me in the right direction. I thank my father, whom I have never met, for *not* being there because it only made me stronger in the end. I thank my most recent father figure, Edward Turner, for always being there when I need him, even though I am not his biological daughter. I thank my husband for being there for me when I was whining and complaining. I love you and thank you for weathering the storms with me since the age of 14. And even when I was there physically but not mentally, thank you for your understanding and patience. I thank my boys and baby girl for keeping me busy all day, every day! I love you all and know that God will take you to great heights. Aunt Izzie, thank you for saying things were alright, even when they weren't alright. To my host of uncles, aunts, friends and extended family, thank you for believing in me and pushing me to be what I am today. God bless you all!

To Bishop Charles H. Ellis III, pastor of Greater Grace Temple and Presiding Bishop of The Pentecostal Assemblies of the World, thank you for your spiritual leadership and covering you have provided down through the years. Thank you for always being in arm's reach and for being available whenever I needed you. Thank you for being an awesome pastor and counselor in times of trouble. I hope I make both you and God proud as I endeavor to feed those who are broken, in and outside of the Kingdom. Thank you for your words of encouragement through your many messages and illustrated sermons. I pray God blesses you and the first family with all of the desires of your hearts. I love you!

Lastly, thank you, the reading audience, for picking up this book. There are many inspirational, encouraging and uplifting books on the shelves. I feel honored that you chose this one to spend your valuable time reading. I pray it meets you right at the point of your need. I pray it ministers to those of you who are depressed and feel oppressed through your tests and trials. Rest assured that God is still God, today and forevermore, and He loves you. Even though it may seem He is not there, He's right there with you in the midst of the fire. Trust Him and seek Him in all that you do, and He will step in on time! God bless you and I pray that you get what you need from God ministering to you through this book.

I did.

Death Before Life

I considered it many times in my life. It was the easy way out. It would make things better. I would be at peace and have no more worries. Suicide. Life didn't get any better than what it was at that point. I was stuck in a trance and death was the only solution to the problem. I had heard of people hanging themselves in closets and in their basements and their families finding them hanging there days later once the suicide act had already been committed. I was too scared to do it that way, though. I had also heard of people overdosing on aspirin or Motrin. But that was too simple—to just take some pills and never wake up again and keep the family wondering how I died. Some people, mostly men, of course, would simply shoot themselves in the head or in the mouth so they would simultaneously pull the trigger and yet, not live long enough to feel any pain. I never liked pain though, so I couldn't take the chance that I might actually have felt the bullet pierce my face. None of those seemed like good choices to me. Those were my choices but, as you can see, I lived to tell the story.

Most people who consider suicide are at a point in their lives where nothing seems to go right. Everything seems to be in disarray and they seem to have lost hope. Bills are past due. The price of gasoline and groceries are skyrocketing like never before. Companies that have kept thousands of workers employed for over 20 years have made cutbacks, which send many into the financial battle of their lives. Creditors are calling daily, requesting payments on debts you never knew you were creating in the first place. Mortgage rates are fluctuating higher and higher, while property values are plummeting to an all-time low. Schools are closing down for lack of funding and student enrollment. Insurance rates and home property taxes continue to increase, even though the foreclosure list remains too extensive to count.

For the person who has never once thought of suicide, you can't even fathom why a person would take his or her own life. To you, he or she may seem like a weak person, or a person that has made many mistakes in life and just wanted to finish the course. But in reality, some people who have committed suicide were pretty strong-minded, well-known celebrities. Some had plenty of friends and family and the money to take care of the host of friends and family, as well. I once heard someone say that rich people have problems, too. Tell that to a broke person. In the midst of a financial storm, all a broke person can see is financial lack. But a rich person can be diagnosed suddenly with cancer and give up on life right then and there, and all of his or her wealth and money is left here for the family to fight over. When I was a teenager, I thought money could buy anything. As I grew up, I found out it couldn't buy true love. It couldn't buy a true friend. It couldn't cure cancer and AIDS, and it surely couldn't make a marriage work. So, if you were considering suicide because of your lack of money, think again.

It was October 19, 2003 when I married my husband, whom I had dated off and on since I was 14 years old. This seemed like the happiest day of my life. It seemed like the right thing to do. We were recently saved and active in the church. We lived together, or 'shacked', as saved and sanctified folks like to call it, but we tried to refrain from sexual activity until marriage...I said we tried! The wedding was beautiful, complete with friends and family from near and far. The reception was the best part of it all! The family-style dinner, the first dance, photos outside at the gazebo, and an open bar for those who drank much more than they could pay for. It was hard to hustle in my four-layer gown, but I managed to kick it anyway. After all, this was my celebration and I wasn't about to let twins stop the show. Yes, I was five months pregnant with twins at the time.

That night, we were exhausted. I went home, took off the wedding dress and flew to the restroom. That meatloaf and ham didn't agree too well with wedding cake. Plus, the twins were probably a little shaken up from all the movement throughout the busy day. The next morning, we went and had breakfast with the groomsmen who had come from out of town. I was off work until Tuesday, so we just hung out until we had to take a few friends to the airport that evening. At 8 p.m., we met my new father-in-law, who was still in town from the wedding, for dinner at Nikola's. We met them at the table, as they were already seated, and I excused myself to go to the restroom. (Being pregnant makes you go a lot more than you want to.)

Once inside the stall, I went to use the bathroom only to discover that I was passing small blood clots. Something was seriously wrong. I ran out of the restroom to tell my husband we needed to leave and go to the hospital. As we drove to Providence Hospital, it seemed like eternity. My stomach was beginning to cramp harder, and I constantly felt like I had to use the bathroom.

When we arrived in the emergency room, I was taken to a room where the nurses elevated my feet. I was having contractions and didn't even know it! The elevation of my feet was supposed to help stop the labor. After the doctor came in and "checked" me to see how far dilated I was, they told me that if the twins were born at that point, they would risk having cerebral palsy and other birth defects. They also told me that even if the twins came out alive, they would not do anything to keep them alive. I had to be at least twenty-four weeks in my pregnancy in order for them to be placed on life support until they could breathe on their own. I was only twenty weeks. This meant that even if my babies were born alive, they would die sometime shortly thereafter. The thought of that sent my mind spinning in hundreds of directions. Sure, I was nervous about having to deal with two babies at once. But the thought of losing them was even more frightening than the thought of having to raise them until the age of eighteen.

The contractions slowed down slightly, but it wasn't enough. Early on October 21, 2003, I gave birth to the first twin, which was a girl. She was born alive, and doctors quickly tried to hand her to me to hold. Knowing that she wasn't going home with me, I refused to hold her. Doctors took her over to the table to clean her up. They then put clothes on her and took a few photos. For a minute, I had a moment of false hope that she would live because surely, she came out breathing on her own and God, being who He is, would not let her die. But shortly after the photos were taken and the family had come in the room to console me, she was gone. The scary thing is that one of the photos taken by the doctors actually shows the moment in time when her spirit left her body. It almost looks like a double image of the body, but a fainter photo of her tiny corpse. She weighed less than one pound when she was born and was only here for maybe an hour. But in that small amount of time, she had taken her first pictures, breathed her first breath, was introduced to most of the family, and was out of here.

We named her Faith Maylee. The middle name was actually a combination of both of our grandmothers' middle names: May and Lee. Sounded country, but she wouldn't be here to question us about why she got such a unique middle name. The first name Faith was chosen to encourage myself, since I had learned that faith was the substance of things hoped for and the evidence of things not seen. For the next few months after I lost Faith, it was hard to hear Bishop Ellis preach on faith. Just the mention of the word faith would send me into emotional whirlwinds. I couldn't understand why God would let such a thing happen the day after my wedding. I had heard of God raising people from the dead and healing the sick. I had also heard of babies being born very prematurely, yet in the end, living a normal life as though they were born on their original due date. So why was my case unsolvable by God?

There was a small memorial service for Faith held in the chapel of the hospital. Of course, the body wasn't there, but there was a little wicker basket with a plush doll inside that sat at the altar. Many friends and family came over to me to console and encourage me, but at this time, I just wanted to be left alone. Hearing that is was going to be alright and that my 1-hour old child was in a better place didn't help me to be at peace. I just wanted this memorial service to be over so I could go back to my hospital bed and rest. My body needed rest, but more than that, my mind needed rest. I wasn't eating much and definitely wasn't sleeping much. I stayed in the hospital about a week after the loss and was sent home on bed rest. Since I was still pregnant with the other twin, I had the chance to go full term with the second twin…or so I thought I did. Maybe three or four days later after I was sent home from losing Faith, I was rushed back to the hospital.

This time when I went into the hospital, they immediately informed me that this twin would not make it full term either and that I had two choices-to induce my labor and get it over with or let the situation play out on its own. Of course, I didn't want to lose this baby after losing the other one a week ago, so I chose to let the pregnancy play out to see what would happen, only to have doctors "check" me and tell me I was being forced to induce my labor and it was nothing else that they could do. This was it. Tears began to flow again. Not only out of sadness, but out of anger. This was supposed to be a joyous time in my life. I had just married not even two weeks ago! We didn't have the funds for an elaborate honeymoon, but we certainly didn't plan on spending it in a hospital room.

I gave birth to the second twin, and the nurses placed him on my chest, only for me to almost have a nervous breakdown. I was crying out loud and screaming on the inside, trying to figure out why God would allow two babies to come into the world for yet a moment, and then take them away. At the time, I wasn't trying to hear, "The Lord giveth, and the Lord taketh away." I didn't want to hold this baby either because again, he couldn't go home with me. That would be like giving a child a piece of candy but telling him or her you need it back. Good luck! I don't recall if Jeremiah Mykel lived longer than Faith or not, but I remember being taken into surgery to have both placentas removed since they were not pushed out from birthing the babies. When I awoke, I was on a hospital bed covered with warm blankets, not remembering any part of the surgery, except looking at the ceiling lights counting backward from ten. I asked my husband how the baby was doing, and just in that short amount of time, he too had made his cameo appearance and was gone.

There was no memorial service for Jeremiah. I couldn't sit through another emotional imaginary funeral for babies who became angels before they even took their first steps. Life wasn't fair. I had friends who didn't even want kids that had plenty. I heard them complain about how their kids got on their nerves and how they weren't having any more, only to watch them become pregnant again the next year. And ironically, all of their pregnancies were successful. And they weren't even married! I felt like God was punishing me for my sin while He was letting them have all the fun in the world, producing more kids than they actually wanted. And here I was, dying inside spiritually, emotionally and physically, because of the sudden tragic loss. It's funny how those who have no desire to have kids always end up pregnant, usually more times than they expect. This was my first pregnancy, and I could see God taking one and leaving the other to fill in the gap for the both of them. But both of my babies, whom I had carried for five months, were gone.

I wasn't super spiritual then, and I am not where God quite wants me to be yet today, either. Back then, I knew a little of the Word, but I wasn't reading my Bible to know God for myself. I hadn't spoken in tongues, and I didn't always understand what caused people to run around our huge edifice called a church. It wasn't until a few years after the loss that I figured out why I lost the twins. It was not by happenstance that I lost them the day after my wedding. Many thought that was the sole reason we were marrying anyway. In a sense, God was saying, "If you got married only because you were pregnant, this is the point where you leave." This was a test to see what the marriage was really built on. Many times, the thought crossed my mind to get an annulment after the loss. But God had to prove a point to me that He honors marriage and takes the covenant relationship very seriously. I knew that if I left, those who had assumed that the marriage was built on a pregnancy would have been right in the end. We had planned to get married anyway, so we just accelerated the process.

This sign was also from God: in all things, we need to wait on Him. Sometimes, we want things for all the wrong reasons. God, Who already knows our ending, is trying to put the brakes on us while we are moving 100 miles per hour right into a danger zone. Had we waited on God, the twins may be alive today. There wouldn't have been a reception or wedding plans, which added extra stress to an already stressed pregnancy. I wished somehow that God could have let Faith and Jeremiah live and take me in their place. But I was left with the painful memories of going through labor, a labor that seemed somewhat all in vain. I was left with memory boxes filled with photos, small footprints and death certificates. Depression set in for many months, and my life was just not where I wanted it to be. I had lost a part of me somewhere along the way, not only because I lost the twins, but also because I lost a part of my spirit, my mind, my peace, my joy. Everything had moved so fast that I couldn't remember where to go and gain it all back.

I was going out of my mind. Prayer couldn't bring me out. Fasting couldn't pull me back into my joy, and words of encouragement only sent me into deeper levels of depression and crying spells. I had never had a nervous breakdown before, but this sure felt like a mini-version of one. But I was saved. I was fed with the Word weekly at church and listened to many worship CDs while riding in my car. Surely, something had to minister to me at the point of my need!

But instead, I was slowly breaking down from the inside out.

Tenita C. Johnson

A Long Way from the Proverbs 31 Woman

When my husband and I married, I was twenty-three years old. I thought I had all it took to be successful in my marriage. I don't know why I thought that. I was raised by a single mother and never knew my father, so I didn't have any example of what a marriage should be like. I thought it would be quite fun to be married. The Cosbys had fun. No matter what the problem was for that particular episode, they always overcame it within that thirty-minute segment. I soon learned that it was impossible to solve any *real* problem in thirty minutes.

My husband stayed on the road a lot with his job in the beginning. This put more strain on the marriage than I thought it would. That crap about absence making the heart grow fonder didn't work for me. I was newly married with preconceived notions about what my marriage should have been like…and it wasn't supposed to be like this. It was supposed to be full of family road trips and walks on the beach. It was supposed to be full of weekend family activities, praying together and movie nights on the couch. Instead, my life was balanced between working from 4 p.m. to midnight at AT&T, getting up five hours after I had just laid down to take my stepson to school, heading back to sleep from 9 a.m. until about 2 p.m., and getting up to do it all over again.

My husband was gone most times during the week, but he would always come back on Friday night or early

Saturday morning for the weekend, only to leave back out early Monday morning on the first flight out of here going on to the next job. He had a little time off in the beginning because of the wedding and then the sudden loss of the twins, but he had to return to the road. I was cool with that or at least I thought I was.

Reality soon set in that I was alone. I was married, but was physically alone. The twins were gone. My husband was gone most of the time. And I didn't spend much time with my stepson because I worked at night and he went to school during the day. This was marriage? What happened to the fun? I was supposed to be planning family getaways and falling in love all over again. I was instead making plans for someone to pick up my stepson from school…and we won't even speak on the false hope of falling in love again. I guess I had a fairytale idea about what marriage was. I was told it's every woman's dream. Well, once you get in it, it remains just that—a dream.

I'm an only child, so I will admit, I'm a little spoiled. I wanted the attention of my husband, physically. I didn't care that he had to work to pay the bills. Talking on the phone every night wasn't good enough. Seeing him on the weekend was definitely not enough time to build a strong marriage. This was whack. I didn't sign up for this. I said 'yes' and 'I do' to the fun relationship we had while we were dating, not this boring lifestyle. Once again, a state of depression set in.

My life was routine with no room for flexibility or creativity. I found myself wishing I could just rewind the hands of time and change my mind about the whole situation. To make matters worse, my husband eventually had to start staying over the weekend to finish certain projects. So not only was I not seeing him during the week, but now he wasn't here on the weekend either! God had a lot of explaining to do. I knew I hadn't signed up for this. I asked God to check my paperwork. This was a 'paper' marriage.

When I joined my sorority, Sigma Lambda Gamma, in college, we went through our unique pledging process and then were inducted into the sorority. But when we took road trips, we found that there were chapters who had what we called 'paper' status. This meant that these chapters had paid the necessary money, but did not go through a pledging process, but yet were able to wear the Greek letters and enjoy all benefits of being a part of the organization. In the world of sororities and fraternities, 'paper' status is not respected. These chapters are looked down upon by those who actually went through the process and earned the right to wear the letters, for the pledging process helps build the sisterhood and bond between the line of prospects so that when they 'cross,' nothing can separate them from the sisterhood.

We didn't have that process in the beginning of the marriage. It was all work and no play. After all, how can you build a successful marriage and relationship with the barrier of long distance? Soon, my loneliness turned into anger.

My husband would call and I wouldn't have much to say. He knew my daily schedule, so why would he call and ask, 'What did you do today?' There was nothing to talk about unless he was calling to talk about coming home. I remember him calling one time from the airport when he was on his way home. By this time, his coming home didn't excite me any. I knew he was only here for a season, i.e. two days, and away he would go again. But this time was different.

I explained to him in so many words that I was not happy. The distance did not make me love him more; it actually made me have a strong dislike for him. It sounds selfish, but at the time, I didn't get married to spend all of my days alone. I knew he had to work, but there were other jobs he could get where he wouldn't have to travel. All I wanted him to do was to start looking for another job so he could be at home. Instead, he called his boss immediately and informed him that he would not be returning the next week to complete the job he had started when he was out of town. At first, I thought he was just taking vacation time, but he had actually quit his job!

I couldn't believe it. Why would you quit a job without having another one to walk into? At the time, I wasn't impressed. Many said that had to be an ultimate love, but I felt like it was ultimate stupidity. I mean, we had bills to pay. After all, he was supposed to be the head. How can you be the head when you have no job to provide for your family? This alleviated the stress of being away from each other for long periods of time, but now there was added stress on me since I was the only employed person in the home.

This took place long before I figured out that marriage is about sacrifice. I couldn't understand why he did what he did back then, but in the end, I've come to know that it's all about the sacrifice. I didn't appreciate it then, but I understand it more and more as time goes on. He was willing to do whatever it took to make the marriage work. I can't say that if the shoe was on the other foot, I would have quit my job for the benefit of the marriage. Well, at some point, I did. (But that's a whole other chapter.)

I didn't know how to be a wife. There weren't too many married women in my life while I was growing up, so examples of what a wife should be were far and few. I thought it was like having a baby—once you gave birth, everything else would come out of natural instincts. Was I ever wrong. I didn't know the first thing about being married. I thought it was just like being boyfriend and girlfriend, only we now had a legal piece of paper binding us so there was no option for breaking up. Breaking up would now be called legal separation or divorce.

I never liked cooking either. I was always a person who liked to clean. I didn't have a problem washing dishes, dusting, sweeping, and vacuuming. But slaving over a hot stove was not my style. I was born in Chicago, so I didn't know anything about the down-home southern cooking that southern people talk about. Don't get me wrong, I had a grandmother who knew how to throw down in the kitchen, but she made her transition before she could pass the recipes onto me. So the most I knew how to do, the right way, was fry some chicken or pork chops and open a can of vegetables and a box of instant rice. Sounded like a good meal to me, until I married someone who was used to eating meals made from scratch on a daily basis. I used to think making a cake from scratch meant opening the cake box that was bought at the store and adding eggs and milk. I knew nothing about sifting flour three to four times, then sifting the sugar that many times or more to get large crystals out that I never noticed when I was using sugar to make Kool-Aid. That all just took too much of my time to even try and learn when I could just go buy the mix and have a cake baked in no time.

Then, I realized I was the one responsible for cooking for the entire family. I guess I was under the impression that because I married someone who could cook very well, he would just gladly take over that chore. I didn't cook often, but whatever I did cook was fried. Fried chicken. Fried pork chops. I really thought I was doing something by opening a can of corn and a box of wild rice, until my husband started complaining that I cooked the same thing all the time. I was offended. Here I was, trying to cook what I knew how to, ensuring that it was safe for the family to eat, and he was asking for variety. I started blaming the world for my lack of knowledge. It wasn't my fault I didn't know how to cook like he wanted me to. Or was it?

I didn't want to change. I felt like I shouldn't have to change because he said "I do" just like I did, and if he really didn't mean it, then that was between him and God to work out. Plus, if I changed, that somehow meant he had control over me. It was almost like whatever he requested of me I had to do. That would be like a servant-master relationship, and no one wants to be treated like or referred to as a servant. The world looks down on a servant. It is the lower position of the two titles: servant and master. I wanted to be the master, or at least a co-master if he was going to be head of household (HOH). But I definitely did not want to be anybody's servant. I was raised to be strong and independent, while servants are raised to depend on their master for everything. Nope. That characteristic didn't fit my resume. I couldn't depend on anybody else for anything. I couldn't be caught with my guard down. I was taught that people will always fail you and let you down at some point. So don't give them a chance to.

Then, God revealed to me that I was indeed a servant to my husband, and vice versa. For some odd reason, when I got married, I thought it was about my being happy, and I oftentimes found myself being so far away from that goal that I thought it was impossible to achieve. This wasn't fun like it was when we were dating. What was so exciting about doing laundry, washing dishes, cooking and cleaning up behind kids constantly? What had happened to the trips we used to take alone for weekends at a time? What happened to those days when I dreamed of waking up next to him? It had all come to pass, but it was not all that my mind had made it to be…until one day, I read a book entitled *Every Woman's Marriage* by Shannon & Greg Ethridge. Many times, we as married people are always praying for God to change our spouse into what we want them to be. But if you really seek God and pray, in due season, He will answer your prayers; it just may not be the answer you expected to receive. God will usually cause you to examine some things about yourself, instead.

It was after reading this book that I realized that marriage takes hard work. Some people say they would rather work a 9-5 every day than be married because the work is that much harder at home. I also learned that marriage is not about making yourself happy. Surprised? Yeah, I was, too, when God revealed it to me. It's about making the other person happy. Through life's circumstances, I have learned that it really is much more of a blessing to give than to receive. This rule applies to our lives. We can't base what we give to our spouse on what he or she gives to us. It's not a competition; someone will always come up short. I learned that marriage means doing some things you may not feel like doing. It means going the extra mile when you feel you don't have anything left inside of you to push. Most of all, it means humbling yourself and putting aside foolish pride. This can be the hardest challenge for married couples because no one wants to be the first to say "I'm sorry" or "I was wrong." In God's eyes, the greatest person is the one who chooses to humble him or herself. It doesn't really matter what other people think or if your spouse views you as the weaker person. Sometimes, being the weaker person means being the stronger person in the relationship. God sees you and God knows your heart. You cannot decide how you will act toward your spouse based on the way he or she treats you.

The Word of God tells us in I Corinthians 7:34, *The unmarried woman cares about the things of the Lord, that she may be holy both in body and in spirit. But she who is married cares about the things of the world-how she may please her husband.* This means that while God is still priority in your life, your husband now becomes a top priority as well. Pleasing your husband is not always an easy task, but through the help of God and much fasting and prayer, it will be revealed to you what you need to do to be pleasing in his sight. Ephesians 5:22-23 says, *Wives, submit to your own husbands, as to the Lord. For the husband is the head of the wife, as also Christ is head of the church.* Many misinterpret and twist this powerful scripture because they assume that submission is doing whatever your husband tells you to do, without any questions or concerns. And because some married men choose to beat women over the head with this scripture, many women believe submission applies even if the relationship is abusive and corrupt.

If they read the next verse, which compares the husband to the wife as Christ's relationship with the church, many men may not quote the scripture as much. Knowing God and who He is, we know that Christ loves the church. We know that He is kind, patient and merciful to the church. Even though God lays out certain commandments for us to follow, God gives us choices in life. So when men 'put their foot down' and use the 'submission' verse, they need to be careful. It doesn't mean a husband ruling over his wife, leaving her with no voice in the home or relationship. The Word of God tells us the woman was created as a help meet. This means that the two walk as one, and even if the husband has the final say-so on certain issues, it is understood that he has consulted or at least discussed the issue with his wife beforehand. Women overlook a critical part of this scripture, too. The part where it says submit to your husbands is important; but more importantly, the charge is to submit as you would submit unto the Lord. So, women, I challenge you today to fully submit to your husband. In your obedience, it may seem like you are giving honor to him, but you are really giving more honor to God. No matter what your husband is doing or not doing, it is still your responsibility to hold up your end of the deal. If God stopped blessing you today, would you stop praising Him? If He didn't give you the answer you were looking for or the job you wanted, would you still serve Him? If you answered no, the same applies to your marriage. It doesn't hurt to adopt a spirit of servitude toward your husband. It's the little things that could make a huge difference.

Ephesians 5:25 charges husbands to...*love your wives, just as Christ also loved the church and gave*

Himself for her. When you think of how good God has been to us, who wouldn't praise Him? The ultimate sacrifice of love was His dying on the cross for our sins. But, this is how much God expects the husband to love his wife. That means unconditionally, through all her secret faults and mishaps, mistakes and mess ups, bad attitude and bad shape. If God chose to die on the cross for only a certain amount of us based on our attitudes or body size, we would all be out of luck because no one is without sin. So when God charges the husband to love the wife *just as* Christ loved the church, make sure you are up for the challenge. And know, husbands, that if you love your wife to the extremity that Christ loved us, she has no problem with submission. If each person in the marriage is giving wholeheartedly to the other person, both can't help but be happy.

But before I knew all of this, my take on the Proverbs 31 woman—expressed through verses 10-28— was as follows:

Who can find a virtuous wife?
(What the heck does virtuous mean? And he didn't find me, I found him.)

For her worth is far above rubies.
(Is that more or less than a diamond's worth?)

The heart of her husband safely trusts her;
(I think he trusts me, with strong caution, not safely.)

So he will have no lack of gain.
(Shouldn't this be so *we* won't have no lack of gain?)

She does him good and not evil;
(Let him tell it, I'm always evil! What if I meant to do good, but it turned out to be evil?)

All the days of her life.
(We won't make it to the end of this year, let alone all the days of my life!)

She seeks wool and flax;
(For what?)

And willingly works with her hands.
(I didn't mind working, but not with my hands at all.)

She is like the merchant ships, she brings her food from afar.
(I hope I don't have to go that far for food! I'll go around the corner but not out of the country for food!)

She also rises while it is yet night;
(Only when God woke me up many times and would not allow me to go back to sleep.)

And provides food for her household,
(Who is cooking in the middle of the night?)

And a portion for her maidservants.
(I don't have any maids or servants but if I did, they would be cooking for me.)

She considers a field and buys it; from her profits she plants a vineyard.

(I would buy the property, but I have never been one to work in the yard.)

She girds herself with strength, and strengthens her arms.
(I could work out sometimes, I guess.)

She perceives that her merchandise is good, and her lamp does not go out by night.
(Anything I'm selling has got to be good simply because I made it. Why wouldn't the lights go out by night? I'm supposed to sell around the clock?)

She stretches out her hands to the distaff, and her hand holds the spindle.
(I had no clue what this meant.)

She extends her hand to the poor, yes, she reaches out her hands to the needy.
(Sure, I don't mind helping the homeless and poor when I have extra to spare.)

She is not afraid of snow for her household, for all her household is clothed with scarlet.
(If scarlet is as heavy as a fur coat, then I guess I wouldn't be afraid of being kept warm.)

She makes tapestry for herself; her clothing is fine linen and purple.
(That's cool I guess; I like purple clothes.)

Her husband is known in the gates, when he sits among the elders of the land.

(He is pretty well known in the church.)

She makes linen garments and sells them, and supplies sashes for the merchants.
(I don't even know how to sew, let alone making whole garments that are worth some money.)

Strength and honor are her clothing; she shall rejoice in time to come.
(I want to be strong, but how long will *in time to come* take?)

She opens her mouth with wisdom, and on her tongue is the law of kindness.
(I can't say that everything that comes out of my mouth is wise or kind.)

She watches over the ways of her household, and does not eat the bread of idleness.
(I'm always watching everyone in the house, husband included. I'm just nosey like that.)

Her children rise up and call her blessed; her husband also, and he praises her:
(Please, they call me evil and mean, and so does he.)

Then God revealed to me how ignorant and clueless I was and that it wasn't all about me.

Tenita C. Johnson

It's Not All About You

It was February of 2007. We had just completed consecration and a week of fasting and praying at my church. It was a new year, one that was declared to be "The Year of Release." I was looking for mine. I was still working at AT&T as a proofreader for the yellow pages division. My husband was working at the job he got once he quit his other job because of my selfish needs—Pfizer Pharmaceutical. We both had "cushiony" jobs that paid well, but didn't always require hard labor, sweat and tears to get the job done. We had heard of the economy getting worse, with employers cutting back on jobs and laying off workers left and right. It became a daily part of the nightly news. If it wasn't Ford, it was Chrysler. If it wasn't Chrysler, it was Delphi, and so on. Hearing it on the news made me numb to the fact that unemployment actually affected real people who have real homes with real bills—until the epidemic hit my home. I received a call from my husband telling me that they would not only be laying off the contractors, which is what he was at the time, but that the entire Ann Arbor site of his job would be shutting down for good. It was mind boggling to think that we had just gone through his being unemployed for six months when he quit his job after we married; now we had to deal again with the uncertainty of when and where he was going to work. The search began as usual. Daily job searches on the computer kept the system tied up for hours at a time. Even after spending many hours and days searching online for employment, he was lucky if one interview came out of it all. And oftentimes, that one interview didn't lead to a job because either he was overqualified or it wasn't something he was interested in doing. He was taking the news well, but I wasn't. Or maybe it was just a front to keep me thinking he had things under control. I didn't understand why God had chosen to pick us out from the crowd and allow this epidemic to hit our home. After all, we had two kids, a mortgage, two car notes, and not to mention the frigid $400 bills the light and gas company sent every month, expecting the entire thing to be paid in full by the time the next billing cycle rolled around. We were faithful in the church. We paid tithes and offering. We always fasted and prayed when Bishop instructed us to. We always gave whenever a special offering was called for. We were even active in various ministries throughout the church. But none of that mattered when we got the layoff notice.

I soon learned that it's a lot easier to tell someone else to pray whenever they are going through a tough situation; but when it came down to practicing what we preached and what's been preached to us, that was a different story. I had faith that prayer could change anybody's situation—but my own. I believed God could heal the sick from cancer and AIDS. I believed that He could make a way out of no way for a person that needed food on their table for next week. I believed that those who rode around with their gas gauge on E would soon be blessed with gas money and not be stranded by the side of the road. I often prayed and interceded for many friends and family members, whether they asked me to or not. Especially after I got married, praying for other people's marriages became a nightly prayer because I not only heard their complaints and grief, but knew firsthand the struggles my marriage had been through (and is still enduring today). I asked God the all-famous cliché question: "Why me?" only to have my question answered with a question: "Why not?" After all, who am I that I have been so great and righteous that God should spare my household from being hit with spiritual storms? Then the question became, if my husband was to be the head of the household, why was he always the one being unemployed in the marriage? Why didn't I ever get the chance to sit at home and collect unemployment? Asking that question was probably the biggest mistake and accomplishment I have made all at the same time in my life.

A company called him from Texas, and they flew him there for an interview. We had always discussed leaving the city of Detroit and moving south, but we just weren't sure if this was the opportunity to take or not. He returned from the interview two days later, and not even 24 hours after he got off the plane, he had a call from them with a job offer. I was working on my Master's degree online at the time, so working and maintaining school, along with household chores, was getting to be stressful. So I, not knowing I was putting my foot in my mouth, told my husband that wherever he found a job, I was willing to move and follow him. That meant I would quit my job at AT&T that I had worked at for four years and start all over in a new city where we didn't know anyone. But I had done it before. I went to undergraduate college at the University of Missouri-Columbia, and I didn't have any friends or family when I left Detroit in the fall of 1997. But I soon made friends, some who became like family, got a decent job to maintain my college bills and made it through the transition. So this couldn't be harder than that, right? He asked the company for time to think about the decision. He would have to move first and work 30 days before he could get the moving stipend to move the kids and me down. He asked me what he should do and part of me wanted to go, but there was a small part that feared that if things didn't work out, I would not only be unemployed, but unemployed in a new place I had never tread on before.

After much prayer, we decided he would take the job. It was at that point that I realized that not only was I about to put my foot well into my mouth and down my throat, but also I had to actually practice faith like never before. We made the decision together to make the move, hoping that it would lead to a new start with greater opportunities than those presented with the job market in Michigan. He left before the kids and I did, went down and got a place while working the newfound job. In the meantime, I was still working at AT&T, dreading leaving my cushiony, overtime-paying employment that had sustained me for the past four years. It was weird to even think of being unemployed. I hadn't been unemployed since I was a 17-year-old high school student and all local Winkleman's stores had begun to close, forcing me to apply at places like Boston Market and The Half Off Card Shop. I knew what the Word said about the man being the head of the household and how the husband should take care of the family and be the sole breadwinner. But that was too much power to give to one person, in my opinion. Because I was voluntarily quitting my job to follow my husband, I was unable to collect any form of unemployment compensation. So that left me totally and completely dependent on my husband and God alone.

When the Smoke Clears: A Phoenix Rises

I had never been in such a position before. I always had my own. I often bragged before I got married on the independence I had mastered, without begging or depending on anyone else to provide my needs or wants, for that matter. I depended on God and heard the testimonies of how He had made a way for someone else, how He had come through and healed people who were on their deathbed, how He stepped in right on time and blessed people financially before their last dollar ran out. So I knew secondhand that God was able to do exceedingly, abundantly, above all *others* could ask or think. But now, I had to put this hearsay into faith and action for my own life. To the average person, even to some of the saints, quitting a well-paying job with paid benefits for the entire family, paid vacation and profit sharing checks yearly was just plain and downright dumb. But as stated before, I, in so many words, had asked God for this. I was tired of the HOH always being the one unemployed and didn't understand why God wouldn't allow the weaker vessel (that would be me) to be the one in lack, so that the head could actually be the head and not just have the title. (But please note, even though my husband was unemployed for six months early in the marriage, he was still head of household in God's eyes, whether he could contribute more than I did financially or not. Although I did not acknowledge him as being the head during that time, God eventually put me into my proper place.) So, this is where, "Be careful what you ask for because you just might get it" smacked me in the face.

We moved to Waco, TX in early June of 2007. I had visited for a weekend with him before he started the job and had found a great subdivision where we could build our own new home, with state-of-the-art home décor, for half the price of what it would cost had we built it in Michigan. That was really the only part that sold me on the whole idea. The home we were having built was a three-bedroom house, with built-in Jacuzzi in the master bedroom, along with two additional bathrooms, a kitchen that came with all appliances and a fenced in large backyard. It was going to take six months to build the home, so even though we moved to Waco in June, we had to stay in a townhouse until our new home was completed. It wasn't until I turned into my new subdivision in Waco that I knew this was not going to be my permanent place of residence. Anybody who knows me well knows I don't like bugs, those that fly or crawl, nor do I like sweltering heat and humidity that causes my hairdo to last three days instead of seven. But this was my big leap of faith. I was totally and completely, 100% dependent on God and my husband. And if God didn't come through for us, I knew we were in trouble.

Finding a church home was our biggest concern when we got to Waco. There were plenty of large Catholic and Methodist churches nearby. Every time I rode down the road and saw a church, I prayed that it would be a Church of God in Christ or a Pentecostal/Apostolic ministry. Of course, when I finally did see some churches that fit our denomination and beliefs, they were storefront-type buildings with paint chipping and limited parking. We visited a few of these smaller ministries, hesitant because we knew the teaching and preaching we had been under before. And I can honestly say, they all ministered to me with the messages that came forth, but my husband wasn't sold on any of them. So we began the vicious cycle of going to church one Sunday and skipping the next one until we decided which one we would try next. I was continuing to read through the Bible, as Bishop Ellis had challenged the entire congregation to read through the Bible in one year. And even though we lived in Texas, we still sent our tithes and offering to Greater Grace Temple. We were always taught to sow on good ground so we didn't want to take any chances by sowing into ministries in this new town, which we knew nothing about.

Nevertheless, no matter how much I read my Word, listened to gospel music and tried to stay afloat, the spirit of depression would always find its way to come on me.

I was bored sitting in the house all day, every day. Plus, I wanted a job. After all, I did not go to school for four years to sit at home and be a professional housewife (no disrespect intended to those of you who chose to make this sacrifice for your family). I was going to school online at the time to complete my Master of Business Administration, and my husband wanted me to solely focus on that, but I wanted to work. After all, I balanced work, school, the house and the kids when we were in Detroit. I was three months from finishing and wasn't struggling to get through the program. You can only cook and clean so much before it becomes irritating and to me, demeaning. I reflected on what I had left and the decisions we had made concerning this move. I wished I could turn back the hands of time and just let him go work in Texas for a year or so until he found something back in Detroit. I could have continued to work at AT&T and kept the kids in Detroit at their school, and even continued to attend the same church regularly. Depression sometimes turned into anger. Anger sometimes turned into sadness. This was nothing like I thought it would be. I was educated and well-trained, with many years of experience in my field. Surely, I could find a job quickly in this small town. But all they had to offer was customer service positions, starting on the high end at $8 per hour. Unless you worked in a factory or at the hospital, you didn't have a 'good' job in Waco. You could always work at Wal-Mart, but I was too educated to be a greeter for 'Wally World' as we used to call it in college. Not to mention, my husband knew my education and skills, so he wasn't letting me accept anything paying under the salary he knew I was well worth. Otherwise, as far as he was concerned, I could just sit at home and save money on daycare fees. But at this point, I just wanted to go back.

Back to my job. Back to my house. Back to my family and friends and familiar surroundings. But most of all, back to my church. Never did I think that one could become 'spoiled' at a church. I missed the illustrated sermons that often included live animals, spotlights, confetti, music and glitter and glam. Heck, at this point, I missed the regular Sunday services, where Bishop would preach until he sweated out his shirt, loosened his tie and took off his watch. Not to mention when he got to the peak of his sermons and yelled in the microphone: "Say yeah, say yeah, say Yeahhhhh!" I missed the familiar faces. Singing in the choir. The church picnic. I was a part of an awesome ministry, but it took my leaving to realize that the technology and high-tech advancements we had at Greater Grace Temple should not be taken for granted. And as big as this church is, my pastor always made time for people who needed him. Members could talk to him any time they had a problem or a need. He was never too busy. He found time to counsel, to pray, to bless babies and to lay hands on the sick and shut-in. I wasn't just a number. He knew me personally, and not only me, but my husband and kids as well. So the assumption that because you attend a mega-church, you are just a number and the pastor doesn't know you exist is a lie. I could watch the services on The Word Network, but it wasn't the same as being in the midst.

I prayed nightly for God to give me a job or for Him to make a way for us to go back. But even when I found a job as a customer service/sales representative, I cried every day I went through training, knowing this was not what I wanted to do, and I eventually quit after my three weeks of training. I was settling, and if you search the Bible carefully, God does not tell us to take whatever we can get. It doesn't say, "Settle for less, even though I have called you to have nothing but the best." It doesn't say, "You are the tail now, but in the future you may be the head." The Word tells us that we are already the head, and not the tail. It tells us that we are kings and queens, a royal priesthood. So why is it that we live some of the most defeated lives? God made it very simple for me to understand. It's all about faith!

Sure, we can read the Word, quote scriptures and tithe all we want to. But if we don't believe what we read, or what we hear, or what we say, for that matter, we might as well give up now. It took much time before I realized that the entire process—the move, quitting my job, and being in a holding pattern by God—was all to build my faith. I thought it was about me. I had to have disobeyed God somewhere down the line. I had to have cursed myself. Maybe we weren't sowing enough financially. Maybe I wasn't reading my Word enough. Maybe I wasn't praying enough. But then I realized, what good is it to pray for something when you really don't believe God will do it? Not that He can't, but you believe that He won't. As I said before, I believed God could do it for *others*. But when it came to believing He would do something miraculous for me, it was like a fairy tale that never came to life.

My husband soon got a call from the company he had worked for back in Detroit. They wanted him back and needed him desperately. They were still shutting down, but not right away. Not only did they want him back, but they offered him a higher salary to return. I think I started packing before he even said he would accept the offer. After all, I wasn't happy in this place. He wasn't too pleased with this new job either. So it would satisfy everybody to just move back. Most importantly, due to the slump in the housing market, we still owned our home back in Michigan. So we packed up and moved back, and he went back to his old job. I, on the other hand, was not able to get my old job back because I had resigned and my position was not slated to be refilled. I was told I had to wait six months before I could even reapply for any position within the company. That time was almost up; but I was also looking for jobs with other companies. That same depression and anger followed me home and soon, I thought I would never work again. Many told me I was overqualified. Some told me I needed more experience, even though I had the education. Others just flat out told me they couldn't meet my salary requirements. Even when I thought I was close to a new position, the company would either put the position on hold or fill it internally, after making me come in for three and four interviews. My frustration only grew over time…until I got tired of being frustrated, angry and sad over what I didn't have, and focused on God.

I stopped spending 8-10 hours a day on the Internet searching for jobs and began to read my Word more. I read Christian books in my spare time when I wasn't working on school work. Between cooking, cleaning, doing laundry and working on schoolwork, I could keep myself busy enough to not concentrate on the fact that I was unemployed. Every morning, I dropped the kids off at school and picked up a cappuccino from Tim Horton's, then headed home and read my Bible for the morning. It wasn't until I took my eyes off of my situation, and put them on God that my situation began to change. I was a lot happier. I continued to pray, but in a very different way. My prayers changed from asking God to bless me with a job to asking God to let *His* will be done in my life, not knowing that if I would have just stopped fighting against God, His will would have been done a long time ago. I also began to look at the situation in a different light. I was unemployed, but in the midst of that, God didn't let us go hungry. We may not have had everything we wanted, but we always had what we needed. The bills got paid; some of them may have been late, but nothing ever got shut off. We were making it! Not only making it, but on one income when we struggled the last four years on two incomes! Looking at all of that let me know God still had a hand in the situation and He was still in total control. But that was all He wanted from me in the first place. He was trying to get some things out of me. He was trying to humble me, break me, mold me and rebuild me. All the while, I thought he was trying to punish me, when in actuality He was trying to get the glory out of my situation.

It wasn't until I came back to Michigan that I realized that God really has a purpose for everything that happens in our lives. Texas was not a total waste. It was all in the divine plan of the Master planner. We spent a lot of money to get to Texas, and then back to Michigan. I had lost a job. I had lost some friends and even some family members. But there was one thing I did bring back from Texas with me that could not be bought with a job. It couldn't be taken away by friends and family members. That was the gift of the Holy Ghost with the evidence of speaking in tongues. As I reflected on the situation, I realized that if God's sole purpose for our moving to Texas was for nothing more than to fill me with His Holy Ghost, the trip was well worth it! Sometimes God has to get us out of our comfort zone to take us to the next level in Him. After exactly a year and a month from the day I quit my job at AT&T, I was offered a job as an editor at a marketing and advertising firm. But this only came because I stopped chasing a job and chased after God.

When the Smoke Clears: A Phoenix Rises

Father to the Fatherless

*Not a day goes by
That I don't wonder why
My father is somewhere in this world
But for nineteen years, has not met his little girl.
There's a gap in my heart
That's existed from the start.
Does he even care,
If I am here or there?
Will he even cry
If he finds I live or die?
Does he have another life,
With other kids and a wife?
Does he even remember he made me?
From far away does he see,
All those shed tears
I cried for nineteen years?
No matter what, I forgive this strange man.
And somewhere in my heart, I understand.
We all make mistakes in life
And it's only right
That the person confesses to mistakes
So it doesn't seem like intentional heart break....*

Tenita C. Johnson

The Void

The enemy has a way of magnifying our problems, as if they are too hard for God to solve. If you watch the seasons of your life, as you come out of one storm, you most likely will go through another, oftentimes a test you didn't pass the first time around. But in my life, it seems that the enemy will use the same thing over and over again to press my spiritual buttons. One of those spiritual buttons is the issue of my growing up without knowing my biological father. Sure, there were many who stepped up to the plate and helped raise me. They filled that void as a child, but that same void returned as I matured into an adult. As a child, I remember wondering if the man who helped make me even knew I existed. If he did know I existed, didn't he want to know how I was doing? Didn't he care about my first steps, my first words, and my first day of school, high school graduation, prom and other milestones in my life? Then again, maybe he didn't.

I remember making up stories about my father in grade school to friends who asked about my mom and dad, knowing deep inside I only knew of a mom that did the best she could and a grandmother that played the role of 'dad' the best she knew how. I always heard the other kids talk about their mom *and* dad, while I tried not to talk about either for fear of people asking too many questions. I didn't understand why it was such a big secret that I didn't know my father. After all, I wasn't ashamed of the fact that I had never met him. If anything, it would have made people feel sorry for me. But I wasn't looking for sympathy. I wasn't looking for an apology from a classmate or teacher. I was looking for a father. And if the 'I'm sorry' wasn't going to come from the horse's mouth, it wasn't going to do me any good.

I always thought life would have been *better* had I known my father. Maybe I would have had more clothes and shoes. Maybe I would have been able to wear more name brand clothes that my cousins always teased me about not having. Maybe I could have gotten those $100 gym shoes from Foot Locker. Had I had all of this, the kids at school couldn't have possibly teased me about my nappy hair and too-dark skin. They wouldn't have been able to 'cap' on me because I would have out-dressed half of them. I daydreamed about his picking me up from school. His coming to my parent-teacher conferences. His buying me a Bomb Pop off the local ice cream truck. But he never called. He never wrote. He never mysteriously appeared at school to pick me up. What happened that could cause this man to choose to have nothing at all to do with me?

As I progressed through life, it seemed like I was the only person in the entire world that had never met his or her biological father before. But, we all know the enemy has a way of making us feel singled out in the crowd. Friends thought I was exaggerating about the whole situation for attention. It seemed impossible to them that a person could grow up knowing absolutely nothing about one of his or her biological parents. Through the years, the words 'your daddy didn't want you' and 'bastard child' continued to ring in my mind from time to time. Not that people had said these words directly to me, but I had heard them used before toward others. I always wondered if I had other brothers and sisters that I also had never met. What if I was walking down the street one day and saw him and didn't know it was him? I wondered what type of life he lived and if he felt being a part of my life would somehow ruin his. Most of all, I pondered the fact that he could possibly be thinking about me just as much as I was thinking about him, but just didn't have the courage to contact me.

Growing up, I was fortunate enough to have many father figures who attempted to fill the void. Even though my biological father wasn't there physically, there still was no need that went unmet. I think I gave the word 'dad' a new meaning when I used it for everyone in my life that treated me like I was their own. There were 'dads' who gave me extravagant birthday gifts. There were 'dads' who made Christmas extra special by showering me with gifts, such as the new pair of purple Patrick Ewing gym shoes and the original Nintendo System. There was a 'dad' that helped pay my tuition to a Catholic elementary school so that I could have a better education than that offered by the Chicago public school system. There was a 'dad' who sent me money to match what I had saved toward the purchase of my first car. There was a 'dad' who helped move me to Missouri to attend college. There was a 'dad' that secretly gave me money when I didn't want to ask my mother for it. There was a 'dad' that made sure I got to high school every morning. That same 'dad' was there to cheer me on in my track and cross country meets when my mom couldn't make them. There was even a 'dad' who took the time to chastise me with a cutting board for skipping school. And I couldn't say 'You ain't my daddy' because at that time, he was. There were 'dads' who I could talk to about issues that I seemed to think my mother just couldn't understand. Even today, I have a 'dad' who looks out for me and I look out for him. He buys gifts for my children as though they are his own grandchildren and is there whenever I need him. Some of my 'dads' were only in my life for a season and have gone their separate ways. Some of my 'dads' have gone on to be with the Lord. Other 'dads' have just lost touch with me through the years. And some are still a part of my life today. But even with all of these people in my life who made life just a little bit smoother, there was still an empty space.

I remember when Bishop Ellis declared 2007 to be "The Year of Release". He instructed the congregation to take note cards and write down seven things we wanted God to do for us that year. We then laid the cards on the altar, and Bishop said a corporate prayer over them. I don't remember all seven things that I wrote down, but I do remember writing down that I wanted to meet my biological father within that year. I had heard the many testimonies of people throughout the congregation. Some people had received new jobs. Others had received new cars and houses. For others, debts had been forgiven. I heard testimonies of family members getting saved and committing their lives to Christ. Some received large checks in the mail. And I was excited for them, but my request was not material, but relational. If God didn't do the other six things on my list, I had to have this one. Even after moving to Texas and back, my husband received a release of debt that we had been paying on for many years. And I was grateful for that. But only God and I knew what type of release I was waiting for. If God had done all these things for other people in the ministry, surely He could grant me this one simple wish. I was tired of sitting through Father's Day sermons wondering where mine might be on this special day designated just for him. The sermons always ended something like "God is the Father to the fatherless on this Father's Day," followed by an altar call for those who wanted to be saved or needed prayer. I was tired of being in that 'fatherless' prayer line. God was going to do it before midnight on December 31, 2007.

But He didn't. I remember sitting through the New Year's Eve illustrated sermon waiting on God to give me an answer, an explanation or have a mysterious man walk up to me in the middle of service and introduce himself as my father. None of that happened either. God had done all of the things on my 'release' list, except that one. It wasn't until January of 2008, during Consecration week, that God gave me a revelation. Bishop Ellis charged us to once again write seven things we wanted God to do for us in 2008. But while he was instructing us, he said something he had not said the previous year. One thing he said was pray before you write your requests and make sure it is in God's will for you to have what you are asking for. Secondly, Bishop said if God didn't answer all of your seven things on the list from last year, it either wasn't in His will or you don't need it. It was at that moment that I stopped searching.

Jeremiah 1:5 says, *before I formed you in the womb, I knew you; before you were born I sanctified you.* That tells me that God already knew I would grow up without a biological father, so He had already put some spiritual fathers in place to help me along the way. God had already prepared me for success before I was born, regardless of circumstances that tried to break me down in life. God had already made me an honor roll student. He knew I would graduate at the top of my high school class.

He knew I would graduate with a Bachelor of Journalism, as well as with a Master of Marketing. He knew I would write this book and He also knew you would read it! It was during the 2008 consecration services that I stopped chasing a father that hadn't been there for 30 years and became thankful for a Father that had been there every step of the way. I also began to thank God for my mother who pushed me to the limits. Because of the absence of my father, she instilled in me the art of true independence—depending on no one but yourself and God. She made sure I understood that if you worked hard enough, you could have anything you wanted. Most of all, she made sure I understood that my father's absence was not an excuse for failure, but it was a catapult to success. In essence, God was telling me that the people who walked out of my life are not tied to my success. They can't stop my destiny. They don't determine my future. They can't stunt my growth. Actually, by their walking away, I just may reach my destiny even quicker.

So I no longer wait for my father to go buy me the name brand clothes I lacked as a child; I go buy them myself. I no longer wonder if his knowing me would ruin his life; not knowing me has probably affected his life more than he could have ever imagined. I don't worry about the brothers and sisters I may have that I don't know; I have more spiritual brothers and sisters than I could ever account for in this walk with Christ. Not to mention a host of sorority sisters who love me just for who I am, even though we may be miles away from each other. I no longer wonder if he just doesn't have the courage to contact me; I have the courage to forgive him for not being there. It doesn't matter that he was never there. There was always a 'dad' nearby to make sure I had what I wanted and a Father who made sure I had everything I needed. So for the one father that wasn't there, God gave me twenty more to endure various seasons of my life. For that, I am truly thankful.

I don't know your personal situation, but God does. Maybe you had your father and your mother wasn't there. Or maybe you had both of your parents, but lacked a grandparent or an aunt or uncle. I encourage you to honor those God has placed in your life to fill that void. They may not have the same blood running through their veins as you do, but they are part of the Blood of Jesus Christ. The Bible tells us that we often entertain angels unaware. Every person God places in your life as a replacement for someone walking away is definitely Heaven sent. I urge you to forgive the missing person(s) in your life. Stop spending money on Internet searches that return everybody but the right person you are looking for. Stop putting out missing person searches. Stop spending sleepless nights worrying where they are and what their life is like without you. Everything happens for a reason. If God wanted them to be a part of your life, they would be with you today. Many have been a father to this fatherless child, but only one Father has been there since the beginning and is guaranteed to be with me at the end. What didn't kill me made me stronger. But try to explain this to a fourteen-year old boy....

Tenita C. Johnson

When My Definition Changed

Nothing could have prepared my family for this storm. It hit us like a brick that had fallen out of the sky. There was no warning. There was no sign. A simple message that she was gone shook our lives like an earthquake. It is funny how you may wonder about God's purpose, and then one day, when He hits you with it like a brick over the head, suddenly everything makes sense and humility and meekness rest on you.

My stepson was about seven years old when I married his father, but I had already been in and out of his life since birth. So even though he may not have known me from day to day, he knew me. When I would come home from college, I remember picking him up to go play at my godchildren's house. Even as a kid, he was very quiet. It took a lot for him to smile, and even more for him to cry. He was never a mischievous kid, probably because he had basically been around adults for most of his early childhood. Since the age of five months up until my husband exited the Marine Corps, he lived with my mother-in-law.

He was born in Jacksonville, North Carolina, the city where my husband had been stationed for years. When he was transitioned to live with my mother-in-law, he moved to Detroit, even though my husband was still stationed in North Carolina. This not only caused him to be separated from his biological mother, but five other brothers and sisters he would not grow up knowing. I'm not sure how often his biological mother communicated with him when he was a baby, but once my husband and I married, the communication seemed very minimal to me. Phone calls came maybe once every three or four months. They became a little more frequent around Christmas time or around his birthday, and then were sporadic again until that same time next year.

He never showed his feelings outright about the situation. Maybe he internalized everything. When he was younger, he often asked us if he could call her. Sometimes he got a response on the other end, and sometimes he didn't. Even if he did get an answer, phone calls didn't seem to last long. I had mixed emotions when he would ask to call his biological mother. After all, she wasn't calling him every day or every week to see how he was doing. Yet here he was, a young kid, trying to reach out to an adult for relationship. It seemed very unfair, to him and to our family as a whole.

A part of me knew how he may have felt. I knew how it felt to wonder about a biological parent, where they were and what they were doing. I knew what it felt like to wonder why I was here, and yet they were not in my life. I knew what it felt like to wonder what I was missing. When you don't know one of your biological parents, for some odd reason, you always feel like you are missing something greater than what you have right now. At least, that was the case for me. He never went to visit her in North Carolina, until she called and requested his presence at her wedding when he was eleven years old.

Because of my husband's work schedule, he would go to North Carolina, his first time back since birth, alone. Anxiety and fear suddenly appeared out of nowhere for me. Maybe the same emotions rang true for him as well. But I did not want him to go alone. Even though this woman had given birth to him, she was a stranger to me. Though I had not given birth to him, I considered him to be my son. We didn't have the baby mama drama. He didn't go away to his mom's house every weekend like some kids do. He didn't even go visit every summer for that matter. But this was bittersweet. While it may have made it easier for us to move on as a family, I am sure it killed any potential relationship he could have had with his biological mother, and I did not want that for him. I knew I would give anything to have a relationship with my biological father, and I did not want to withhold that from him. But at the same time, where did that leave me?

For the first few years of marriage, I struggled with where my place was in his life. I knew how to provide for him, like a mother should, but I didn't know how to establish a relationship, especially with a child who knew you were not his biological parent, often said it openly, and even questioned it. I found out that because I didn't have a good relationship with my biological mother and didn't know my biological father, I didn't know how to establish a fruitful relationship with my child. It took me three years to realize this. I felt disqualified. I felt like God had entrusted someone else's child with my care, and I didn't even know why I was chosen. I wasn't even sure that I was willing to say "yes" to God's will at the time. I began to doubt not only my qualification to raise a child, but whether or not I had it in me to be married to someone who had a child from a previous relationship, or if I was mature enough to be married at all.

When the phone calls *did* come, no matter how sporadic, my whole demeanor would change. I felt like he opened up to her much more than to me, even though he lived with me every day; yet, I had to pull teeth to get a

"Hello, Good morning" out of him. Maybe he opened up because he hadn't talked to her in months. But the enemy would often play with my mind, having me think he opened up to her more because she was 'mom' and I was just a fill-in for the time being until she came back for him again, whenever that may have been. It bothered me that she even signed his birthday and Christmas cards "Love, Mom," as if she had been here for every birthday party and Christmas morning. If she was Mom, who was I?

On the flip side of things, when the phone calls *did not* come, in the back of my mind, I criticized her. I felt for him, even though he may not have shown any emotion, even when he acted like he didn't care. He had to wonder why she wasn't calling. He had to wonder why she didn't write or even wonder how he was doing in school. Again, he never voiced this directly to me; this was my own personal thought process based on my own past experience. I wanted to love full out. I wanted to give 120%. I wanted to tell him to forget all about her so I could shield him from the hurt. I wanted him to cling to me. But it didn't seem like he was clinging to anyone at the time. And at the end of the day, fear, uncertainty and unsuccessful results from previous attempts shoved me back into my shell. After all, I couldn't love full out because I didn't know what loving full out required. Did it require more hugs and kisses? Did it require telling him "I love you" daily? Did it require spending more quality time with him one on one? As educated and trained as I am, I can honestly tell you, I didn't know. I didn't know until I got a Facebook message from one of his biological sisters stating that his mother had passed away from cancer.

Suddenly, my feelings didn't matter. I had never met this woman personally; I had only spoken to her on the phone from time to time. But for a long time, the enemy had me thinking this woman was my competition. She was my enemy. She was an outside source who was added stress to my family. For years, I competed with an imaginary person who was not even presently near us. The thought was always in the back of my mind; what if she wants him back one day and what if she ever wants to come visit him here, in my home? The what-ifs weren't even relevant anymore. She was gone. My heart ached for him. I wanted to hug and love on him, but even with this, he showed no emotion. Not in front of us, anyway.

It was a struggle trying to decide whether or not I should go along for the ride to attend the services. I wanted to be there as a support if he needed anything and certainly if he needed a shoulder to cry on, if he ever decided to open up that much. But at the same time, a part of me felt like it may have been somewhat stepping on toes. I wasn't sure whose toes I would be stepping on, seeing as though his biological mother was now deceased, but it seemed like this could be quite awkward. After a spiritual tug-of-war, I decided to go on the trip. The drive to North Carolina seemed to start out like any other road trip, playing old CDs and eating snacks, memorable conversations between my husband and me of our distant past. But as we neared the city of Jacksonville, something came over me that I could not explain. Suddenly, I was in unfamiliar territory. After settling into our hotel room, we went to visit his sisters at their mother's house. They showed him love like I had never seen before. They had only met him once in life, when he had come to North Carolina for his mother's most recent wedding, but they hugged him as though he had lived with them for years and had suddenly been taken away in the middle of the night by strangers. The script had been totally flipped. While I thought all along he would view them as strangers and not open up to them, he did the exact opposite. I was the stranger.

My husband, my six-year old son and I spent a lot of time at the mall, eating at various restaurants and shopping, while my oldest son spent time with his other siblings. For the first time, I felt like we were the other family. I never understood why people put greater emphasis on relationships they have with siblings that are by their mother than the relationships with their siblings by their same biological father. Maybe society set it up that way. Maybe it's an individual decision. I never had any brothers or sisters to know the difference. But it didn't seem fair. Maybe I was just being selfish. So I did my best to be there, but to remain somewhat invisible. But it was hard to stay in the background when I wanted to be there with him every step of the way. At the wake, I was able to hold his arm and be there for him as he approached the casket. But as we took our seats in the funeral home, family was seated on one side, while others were instructed to sit on another, which soon divided us. Of course, my husband and I weren't able to ride in the family car with him to the funeral and even though he was in full view and I could see his every move, he sat on the front row of the church, while we sat four or five rows back from him. He seemed to be handling it all well. He never cried during any of the services, or at least he didn't let us see him cry.

I remember hugging him several times, telling him that I loved him several times, yet trying to not overdo it.

Up until this point in our relationship, we hadn't been very affectionate in our home. My husband and I of course were affectionate with each other. My youngest son was very affectionate with everyone because he was yet still very young and loved hugs and kisses. But my oldest son didn't seem to want the affection...or maybe we just didn't know how to give it to him. It was during this time that God revealed to me that because I had grown up in a home where the words "I love you" were rarely uttered and hugs and kisses were reserved for long distance trips and funerals, how could I possibly know how to effectively show love with true outward expressions? It often felt weird and forced. I didn't want to seem fake, as many people deem someone who shows them affection that is not genuine. I wanted him to know that not only was I there for him right now at this very difficult moment in life, but I had always been there for him and would always be there for him. But more importantly, in a matter of one weekend, God had answered so many unanswered questions.

For many years, I questioned why God allowed me to lose twins the day after my wedding, have two other miscarriages, and yet charge me to raise another woman's child. It was during this weekend I realized God knew before my son was formed in his mother's womb that she would die when he would be 14, and he would need someone to take care of him. I also have to believe if God entrusted his life to me, He felt I was worthy enough to raise him to be the young man God has called him to be. For years, I remember being angry over children I had lost. This weekend, I learned to thank God for the two He allowed me to keep down here with me on earth.

This weekend also took away a lot of the fear of what if. I always feared what the future would be like when he grew up to be an adult. Who would he spend the holidays with? Would he seek a greater relationship with his mother's side of the family and forget all about us? What would high school and college graduation day be like? But God removed the possibility of any what if. I would not have had it that way, but we can't change God's will. Maybe God knew something I didn't. Maybe He knew I wouldn't give 150% with the possibility of 'what if' still in the picture. Maybe he knew spiritually I had one foot in and one foot yet still out, waiting on the results of the future. For years, as often as he questioned my place in his life, I questioned my definition in his life. I wasn't his 'real' mom, as kids say, but we didn't allow the word stepmom in our house, so who was I?

It was on this weekend that God revealed to me that no matter what he ever called me, what he ever referred to me as, I was his mother. I just needed to decide to start acting like it. There was no other. The person who had given him natural birth was now laying in a casket in front of me. But I knew God was able to give him rebirth and that He had strategically placed me in his life for such a time as this. I remember growing up reaching out to many of my mother's boyfriends for the father figure in my life. But even once the man whom I call dad today came into my life, I was quick to tell him that he was not my father and he couldn't tell me what to do. I remember not wanting to follow his rules. I remember not wanting to go anywhere with him. Sure, he bought me nice things, but as a kid, I was only looking for what was in it for me. I wasn't trying to establish any form of relationship with him long term. I wasn't trying to be his daughter, though

God knows I longed for a father to rescue me from somewhere, anywhere! I remember calling him by his first name all of my childhood, which seems so disrespectful now that I am on the receiving end. But by the time I got to college, I not only realized that he helped supply my needs for a good portion of my life, but that he was my father.

He drove my mom and me to my college when it was time for me to go away to school. He was always there when I needed to talk. He never hesitated to give me money when I asked for it (a typical daddy's little girl). Even once I married and had my own kids, he cared for them and provided for them just as much as he did me throughout my life. So needless to say, no, he isn't my biological father, but he has more than earned the title of dad today. And I call him just that. Growing up, I don't remember his ever making a distinction between his biological daughter and myself. I was his daughter whether I agreed with it or not. During this weekend, God began to deal with me to do everything in my power as a parent to nurture, raise, and mold my son into the best man he can possibly be, no matter how he seems to feel about me. At this point in time, God was holding me accountable for another life and an upbringing, and I want to be pleasing unto God. I once heard someone say that people don't call you something until you prove you have become it. You have to prove you are qualified or eligible before you get the title. But I also heard someone say that God calls you what you are before you even become it. This makes sense since He knows your future. I had to learn that God called me a mother long before I was born and long before my children were born. He already knew what my sons would need to get them on the right road to their destiny. I never attempted to replace his biological mother, but God made the decision to replace his mother. Even though we don't always understand God's will and plan, most of the time, we don't have a choice but to go with the flow and see what the end is going to be.

So my name hasn't changed. How he perceives me may not have changed. How he refers to me hasn't changed. And even if my title never changes, if he never calls me mom, I am certain that my definition has surely changed, all in the matter of one weekend. God helped me define the madness within.

Defining the Madness

Many have symptoms of depression and don't even know they are heading into a depressed state. Before they know it, they are stuck in a rut they can't seem to shake. Life stops moving. The situation begins to take a toll on their life, and instead of living and pressing toward their future, they begin to be consumed by the situation at hand. Throughout my research, I felt it was necessary to first define depression so that we as a people can understand the meaning of this state of mind that often chokes the life out of God-ordained destinies.

Merriam-Webster's Online Dictionary defines depression as: *a psychoneurotic or psychotic disorder marked especially by sadness, inactivity, difficulty in thinking and concentration, a significant increase or decrease in appetite and time spent sleeping, feelings of dejection and hopelessness, and sometimes suicidal tendencies **c** (1): a reduction in activity, amount, quality, or force (2): a lowering of vitality or functional activity.* But if we look at the root word *depress*, we get a more accurate description of what the act of depressing actually means: *2 **a**: to press down <depress a typewriter key> **b**: to cause to sink to a lower position 3: to lessen the activity or strength of <drugs that may* depress *the appetite> 4: **SADDEN, DISCOURAGE** <don't let the news* depress *you> 5: to decrease the market value or marketability   of.* (Merriam-Webster.com/Dictionary/Depress)

That is the awesome thing about the dictionary; it gives you multiple meanings depending on the circumstance. So, for example, when we examine the word depression, we get a definition of symptoms more so than what the disorder is. It tells us that sadness, lack of activity, lack of concentration, etc. are symptoms to look for when you are depressed. It also tells us one's appetite and sleeping habits may change. But the next part of the definition caught my attention because it says you will feel hopelessness and sometimes act as though you are going to commit suicide. Breaking down just that part of the definition, we examine the word hopelessness, which Merriam-Webster defines as: *1) a: having no expectation of good or success:* **DESPAIRING** *b: not susceptible to remedy or cure c: incapable of redemption or improvement 2) a: giving no ground for hope:* **DESPERATE** *b: incapable of solution, management, or accomplishment:* **IMPOSSIBLE.** (Merriam-Webster.com/dictionary/hopelessness)

According to this definition, a state of hopelessness means you have lost all hope or expectation to succeed. You feel you can never get out of the state you are in now and your dilemma can't be cured. But a word stuck out to me at the very end of that definition: IMPOSSIBLE! We all know what impossible means—that it cannot ever happen! As Christians, the definition of hopelessness, as well as depression, contradicts everything we are *supposed* to believe!

Philippians 4:13 tells us, *I can do all things through Christ who strengthens me.* This means that with Christ, nothing is impossible. Christ is our strength when we are weak. Psalm 31:24 lets us know to: *be of good courage, and He shall strengthen your heart, all you who hope in the LORD*. This means we should have no fear of anything, for God is in control of every situation, as long as we keep our hope pointed in the right direction. For some of us, all hope has been lost because we haven't put it toward things eternal, but toward things of the natural and of this world. Many have lost hope when they got laid off a job they worked at for 20 years. Some lost hope when their home or car was repossessed. Some lost hope when the doctor informed them they had cancer or AIDS. Others lost hope when they lost a very close loved one. But Jeremiah 17:7 informs us that, *blessed is the man who trusts in the LORD, and whose hope is the LORD.* The Word of God even warns us not to put our trust in things other than God. Psalm 20:7 says: *Some trust in chariots, and some in horses; but we will remember the name of the LORD our God.*

Hopelessness also is the state of falsely believing you cannot be cured and no remedy exists for what you have or what you are going through. But again, the Word of God tells us in Psalm 30:2: *O LORD my God, I cried out to you, and you healed me*. This is written proof that God is a healer of the sick, regardless of the disease or disorder at hand. In this passage, it also puts some of the responsibility back on the people of God. He requires that we cry out to Him and ask for healing. This may be easy to do when we are on top of the world, but when depression begins to set in, how many really remember to call on the name of Jesus? We have the tools in our possession, and it's up to us to utilize what God has given us.

Taking a closer look at the root word *depress*, we learn that it can mean to press down, which again, contradicts the Word of God. He tells us in Psalm 24:9 to:

lift up your heads, O you gates! Lift up, you everlasting doors! And the King of glory shall come in. His Word tells us to keep our heads lifted up. In doing so, your spirit, your state of mind, your attitude and your demeanor will be lifted. The second part of that definition goes a step further to say that when you depress something you cause it to sink to a lower position. So when you fall into depression, you are at a lower position than you were before. But God outlines a different promise for us in Deuteronomy 28:13: *And the LORD will make you the head and not the tail; you shall be above only, and not be beneath, if you heed the commandments of the LORD your God, which I command you today, and are careful to observe them.* When we observe the physical body, the head is above the buttocks, also known as the tail, at all times. So in the spiritual sense, God is saying to the Christian community that you shall be at the forefront, and not behind those of the world. His Word also tells us we shall be above and not beneath. This means your life will always be afloat, never sinking into a lost state. But again, these promises are offered to those who take heed to His commandments and take the Word of God seriously.

Lastly, but most importantly, the definition of depress includes decreasing the market value of something. For example, people often refer to the real estate industry as being depressed. Homes are not selling because of the many people who have lost their jobs. Those who are selling homes are not getting nearly as much as they paid for those homes when they bought them. There are even people who owe more money on their home loan than what the property is actually worth! Imagine paying twice as much for something in a store as the price it is marked to sell for. Being in a depressed state will cause you to feel that you are not of value. You have no worth. You have no purpose. You somehow have depreciated yourself to being of less value than you once considered yourself. But the word of God tells us we do have purpose.

Matthew 5:13-16 tells us, *you are the salt of the earth; but if the salt loses its flavor, how shall it be seasoned? It is then good for nothing but to be thrown out and trampled underfoot by men. You are the light of the world. A city that is set on a hill cannot be hidden. Nor do they light a lamp and put it under a basket, but on a lampstand, and it gives light to all who are in the house. Let your light so shine before men, that they may see your good works and glorify your Father in heaven.* When you become depressed, you lose your flavor or seasoning, as God calls it. When you think of salt, many use salt to add flavor to their food. Therefore, God calls us to add flavor to the earth. If we are not doing this—and we are not if we are depressed—then we are no good to God. The Word of God tells us to let our light shine so that God may be glorified. But if people always see us in a depressed, oppressed, downtrodden state, they won't see light; they'll see darkness. Many may be watching you, and you may not notice that they are because you are stuck in utter darkness. How can you draw people to the light when you continually operate in darkness? People should see your attitude, your demeanor and your actions and know that you belong to God. When they see you consistently maintaining a spirit of peace and joy regardless of what goes on around you, they won't be able to resist curiosity and also give their lives to Christ.

Feeling worthless is different from being unworthy. Many times, we as Christians refer to our relationship with Christ and say we are unworthy of His grace and mercy, and rightfully so. We will never be worthy of His dying on the cross, His shed blood and tears, and the mercy He gives us newly every day. No matter how hard we try, we could never work or shout enough to be worthy of what God gives us. But this does not mean we are worthless. That God chooses to use us proves to me that we all have worth. For the Proverbs 31 wife, God compares her worth to a fine stone: *Who can find a virtuous wife? For her worth is far above rubies.* This lets us to know that the wife holds a pretty tremendous value. Psalm 37:25 reminds us, *I have been young, and now am old; yet I have not seen the righteous forsaken, nor his descendants begging bread.* If God didn't feel we were of any worth, He would not promise to take care of us. He would have planted us here on earth and let the chips fall where they may. This scripture is just the tip of the iceberg as to what God has for us. And if we didn't have worth, God would not outline His promises for us in His Word.

So today, I speak words of encouragement to the depressed and oppressed. If you claim to be a Christian, you can't be sad, for the Word of God tells us ...*do not sorrow, for the joy of the LORD is your strength* (Nehemiah 8:10). You cannot get to a place of inactivity in your life because your Word warns you to...*press toward the goal for the prize of the upward call of God in Christ Jesus* (Philippians 3:14). You should not have difficulty thinking or concentrating, for God promises to keep us ...*in perfect peace, Whose mind is stayed on You, because he trusts in You* (Isaiah 26:3). You could never spiral into a state of hopelessness, for the Word tells us to *wait for the LORD, my soul waits, and in His word I do* hope (Psalm 130:5). You cannot reduce your amount of power and force, for the Word of God tells us...*from the days of John the Baptist until now the kingdom of heaven suffers violence, and the violent take it by force* (Matthew 11:12). You can't possibly be pressed down, for the Word of God informs us very plainly that *though he fall, he shall not be utterly cast down; for the LORD upholds him with His hand* (Psalm 37:24). Discouragement is not an option when God has already spoken to you...*do not fear or be discouraged* (Deuteronomy 1:21). You should always expect positive outcomes and great success with God on your side because he promised: *for I know the thoughts that I think toward you, says the LORD, thoughts of peace and not of evil, to give you a future and a hope* (Jeremiah 29:11). Christians cannot operate in despair, for the Word reminds us *we are hard-pressed on every side, yet not crushed; we are perplexed, but not in despair* (2 Corinthians 4:8). And last, but maybe the most important part of the definition of depression to bury, is the word impossible. *For with God nothing will be impossible* (Luke 1:37).

I made a decision to stop letting the words *depression* and *depressed* define me when I found out God's promises for me. A definition is a meaning for a word or product, in this case, a state. Merriam-Webster also defines a definition as making something definite. And you may think you can temporarily operate in depression and go in and out of tantrums and mini-breakdowns. But the symptoms of depression define that state of being, and that definition often becomes definite. Watch the way you speak, the way you act, your attitude and your demeanor. You have the power to write your life's definition. Don't let the dictionary define it for you.

Tenita C. Johnson

When the Smoke Clears: A Phoenix Rises

Built God-Tough

In the automobile industry, all automakers seek to convince consumers that they are getting the best of the best. As soon as a customer sets foot on a new car lot, salesmen bombard them with the features and benefits of whatever vehicle the customer may seem the least bit interested in. The salesman may highlight the interior leather seats or the power windows and door locks. He or she may take the customer on a test drive to show them how smoothly the car runs on the road. Better yet, if the vehicle is equipped, the salesman may even demonstrate the OnStar or GPS features of the vehicle. But rarely does a salesman take the time to tell a customer what the vehicle is made of. They don't tell you what type of parts are on the vehicle. They won't tell you who manufactured the parts and what country the parts came from, if they were not made in America. Some automobile manufacturers promote the "Made in America" standard, but does that mean the vehicle was simply put together in America or that all parts were both made in and assembled completely in America? Nevertheless, I love the slogan for Ford Motor Company. It simply states: "Built Ford Tough."

Essentially, what Ford is trying to do is distinguish itself in a very unique way from every other automaker. Their slogan doesn't tell you much about the fancy seats or the plush carpet. It doesn't necessarily speak to the sunroof or GPS the car comes optionally equipped with. But what it does tell you is that you should expect to get a vehicle that is built to withstand the wear and tear of the road and highway. The "Built Ford Tough" slogan promotes to the customer that no matter how high the hill, how rocky the road, how steep the incline or how hard one may even hit a pothole, a Ford is designed and built intentionally to withstand all of that and more.

Just like the Ford truck, I was built God tough and didn't know it. For many years, I only judged myself based on my outside appearance. I saw my short stature and my small hands. I focused on my short legs, my skin color, which always seemed to be 'too dark' to many, and my oversized feet, which definitely did not match my body size. After all, who had ever seen a 5-feet-tall woman who wore a size 11 shoe? Let's just safely say it was a rare.

But, let's be clear. The last few chapters were not to print a pity party on paper. They were not to introduce you to some of the skeletons in my closet. But they were to prove to you that I have been built God tough. And so have you. I didn't know what I was made of until God took me through the various tests and I came out on the other end, without a scratch or scar. What I thought would kill me was God-designed to build me. The Word of God is true when it says that God won't put more on you than you can bear (I Corinthians 10:13). He knows just how far to push you to get the right amount of glory, the right amount of honor and praise, without letting it take you out of here. At times, when I felt like I would simply fall down and die, God was right there to carry me.

So imagine that God is the customer and you are the vehicle on the sales lot. But unlike most, He's not interested in your makeup or your hairstyle. He's not judging your quality based on whether you have on the latest name brand shoes or clothing. Even more so, though you may be a man with a six pack and arms made of steel, God may still not be convinced that you are built God tough. God's looking at your track record of what He has taken you through thus far to determine what you are capable of handling in the future. The tests are not setups by God for failure. He is not out to get us. He definitely *always* has the best interest of His people at heart. But in order for us to trust Him all the more, in order for us to be totally sold out for Him, and more importantly, in order to remind us of what God has made us of, He must test us and try us on a continual basis.

Every time I get a new car, my husband is with me. We have purchased many certified used vehicles and lately, even a pre-owned lease vehicle. So he always goes with me to ensure that I don't pick out a lemon based on the outside package of the vehicle. I always look at the color of the car. I look at the features, you know, the sunroof, leather heated and air-conditioned seats and even what the interior lights look like at nighttime. He couldn't care less about any of that. He is more concerned with many of the things I just have not taken the time to understand. He's asking the salesman to pop the hood so he can look at the wiring and the engine structure of the vehicle. He wants to look at the trunk space of the vehicle, since he always makes sure that I have a jack and a set of tools in my trunk in case of a breakdown. He is even intrigued with the tire size of the vehicle. For me, as long as it drives on the road and it gets me from point A to point B, I'm good! But of course, it has to look good. I mean as a woman, it's all about the style and look of the vehicle. None of that matters to him, though. He has worked on cars long enough to know that every car that looks good is not always the best buy for our dollar.

God is the same way. He sees many of us as dressed up, primped, prepared and pampered. But on the inside, He can't use many people because they aren't built God tough. At the first sight of trouble, they curse God or lay down their religion and stop coming to church. At the slightest test, they whine, moan and complain, asking why God has forsaken them and left them out to dry. When God is blessing, all is well; but when God is not pouring out natural manifestations of His power and presence, people lose hope and faith, and question the very religion they claim to believe in. Oftentimes, the simplest attack from the enemy or at the slightest look of things turning bleak, our hearts begin to fill with fear. But it is through these tests and trials that God builds us better, from the inside out. After all, if we never went through anything, what would we need God for? What would we pray for? What would we worship and thank Him for? How would we know He is good if we have never fallen on rough times?

Just as my husband has worked on cars long enough to know a great vehicle versus one that needs a lot of work, God knows when one of His children needs to undergo routine maintenance or construction. For most vehicles, it may be recommended that you change the oil every 3,000 miles. This is a known maintenance requirement that a buyer will have to commit to fulfilling every 3,000 miles in order for their vehicle to run as efficiently as possible. So I like to imagine that God knows each and every one of us individually to the point that He knows when we are due for our scheduled routine maintenance. For some, it may be every two or three months, while for others, He may only feel the need to perform maintenance on once a year. But we all must go through a process of maintenance to preserve the things God has set within us.

We all must go through periods of construction. In the natural world, construction means a lot of one-lane highways, slow traffic and dust. The ground is usually broken up into many pieces, and most times, the purpose of the construction is to make the highway or street lanes brand new, not just to repair them. These streets and highways are at the point to where they are beyond repair, and new ground simply needs to be laid. After so many years or maybe even after so many significant events while walking with Christ, we all must undergo a period of construction. During this period, it may seem that God is taking us through the ringer, but what He is really doing is removing the bad ground, the foul ground, the potholes in our lives, the bumps and the bruises so He may purify us all the more. We will never be perfect, but we can continue to be cleansed, reconstructed and rebuilt by God so that as we grow, we grow not only in age, but also in Him, in His love, in His grace and in His mercy. We can't remain babes in Christ forever. At some point, we have to let go of the bottle, move on from the Sippy cup and mature in Christ so that we may help those who will come into the Kingdom of God behind us. A baby has never been able to help another baby walk. How can you help another Christian in his or her faith walk if you are still crawling? How can you encourage others to trust God when you don't trust Him half the time yourself? Let God be the true potter and lie down and serve as the true clay. Let Him mold you into who He wants you to be, not who you think you want to be.

I used to think God's breaking process was solely to break me down and keep me humble. I thought it was to help me remember where I had come from and how I really wasn't that far away from it at all. But then God began to reveal to me that He never breaks something without a purpose. He also never breaks something or takes something away without rebuilding it better. Of course, He never wants us to get to the place where we think we have it all together and that we have conquered every stronghold and struggle, but He was simply rebuilding me...better! I was born to my mother in the natural, but when I accepted Christ in my life, I was born again, not of the natural, but of the Spirit. I've often heard people say that if God brought you to it, He is more than well able to bring you through it. The Word of God also tells us that God will never put more on you than you can bear. So if He allows it to happen, that means He is prepared to help you along the track to the finish line of whatever test and trial may come your way.

I didn't understand it early on in my walk with Christ, but it becomes clearer and clearer to me each day that God is not breaking just to be breaking, but He is breaking me to build me God tough. Once you are born again of both water and Spirit, the Holy Ghost offers power that we would not necessarily have without a life dedicated to Christ. I remember watching cartoons like *The Hulk*, *Superman* and *Spider-Man*. They all had their own special super powers, but whenever someone was in trouble, they always showed up, no matter how far they may have seemed to be away from the problem. God is the ultimate superhero. He always shows up on the scene to rescue us, to protect us and to shield us from any further harm or danger. The difference is that Superman and Spider-Man were never able to give their power to anyone else. They had to do all of the work themselves. But Luke 10:19 says, *Behold, I have given you authority to tread on serpents and scorpions, and over all the power of the enemy, and nothing shall hurt you.* This means God doesn't have to do all of the work for us. He has imparted His same power, authority and anointing to us so that we can do some things for ourselves.

It is up to us to walk in the authority of this power. Although God gave us the power, although many of us have been built God tough, we yet act like spiritual punks. At the first sight of an attack, we hang up our harps of praise, stop going to church and sit on our gifts. When we encounter a mountain, instead of speaking to it to move out of the way, we sit at the bottom of it, cry out to God asking why He even put the mountain there, and beg Him to remove it for us. Mark 11:23 says, *Truly, I say to you, whoever says to this mountain, 'Be taken up and thrown into the sea,' and does not doubt in his heart, but believes that what he says will come to pass, it will be done for him.* So we're doing one of two things. We are either not speaking to the mountain at all, or we are speaking to the mountain but not believing what we are asking for will come to pass. The sad thing is that even the enemy knows when we speak and yet have doubt in our heart. He knows when we mean business and when we are spiritually weak, but just speaking things out of ritual and religiosity.

If we get a bad report from the doctor, we are taught to speak healing over ourselves. Usually, this consists of us saying something like, "By His stripes, I am healed. In Jesus' name, Amen." But by the end of that confession, the only thing ringing true in your head is the black ink on white paper telling you that you have been diagnosed with cancer. You may have prayed the prayer, and maybe five other believers prayed the prayer alongside you, but because of what the facts say in black and white, you still have doubt. Even though you may know twenty people who have personally been healed from cancer, for some reason, you don't believe that God will do it for you. The doubt is not in God's ability to do it; the doubt is when and if He chooses to do it.

In the state the economy is in, we all may have experienced some instances where bills piled up on the dining room table or the refrigerator began to look a little scarce. And even though we know that *all* things come from God above and that He is the true provider, fear begins to set in. We usually pray something like, "God I need you to make a way out of no way." But what we fail to realize that God cannot make a way until *no other* way exists. As long as you can see your way, God is on autopilot. He is yet blessing, but you may not seek Him as diligently as you would when your heat gets cut off in the middle of winter or when your refrigerator has nothing but baking soda in it. Immeasurable amounts of doubt begin to set in. The bills on the table may serve as shut-off notices, and though we're praying and fasting for God to drop a miracle out of the sky, we yet set up for spiritual pity parties and prepare for the shut-off, instead of preparing for the blessing when God takes care of the bill in full. When you get a chance, take time to watch the birds or the fish of the sea. They don't seem to be the least bit concerned about God providing for them. They are secure in their living habitat and seek out their own food, based on the knowledge God gave them when He formed them. Now, if He takes care of the birds, the fish of the sea, among other animals, how much more is He going to allow someone, made in His image, to lack? The Word of God tells us we are royalty; but oftentimes, because of our spending habits, undisciplined tithing and giving of offering and financial seeds, and desires of the flesh, we live at or below poverty level, and you can't distinguish the life of a Christian with that of someone of the world.

But it's time we take our rightful places in the world *and* in the church. God built us in a mirror of His image, and has given us the same power and authority that He holds. Therefore, we need to not only believe we have been built God tough, but we need to start walking and talking like we have been built God tough. I recall a message from Bishop Noel Jones titled "I Wasn't Built to Break." Plain and simple, God didn't build you to break down after every little test and trial that comes your way. He built you to withstand the many, many attacks that come from every side of the enemy's camp. Not only that, He also has a purpose and a plan for everything you go through. It's not meant to break you. It's meant to build you into a better person. With every test, you grow stronger in and closer to the Lord. You come to know Him in a more personal way, and you essentially become an example of His many unmerited promises.

Tenita C. Johnson

The Day of Rebirth

It never ceases to amaze me how the enemy seems to magnify our problems and make them so much bigger than they are. Because of this, if we are not careful, we will minimize our breakthrough when it truly does come, if we even recognize it has taken place at all. Realize that the breakthrough you are seeking may not come in a big, loud bang. It may not come in the form of a million-dollar check in the mail. It may not be as huge as being healed from cancer at stage four. But each person's level of breakthrough will vary according to his or her own faith. Breakthrough is simply described as any act of overcoming an obstacle or restriction; overcoming something that was holding you back from moving forward. In my lifetime, there have been numerous breakthroughs, but I either minimized them when they took place because they didn't come in the form of something huge, or I didn't realize the breakthrough had taken place at all and totally missed it.

One of my biggest struggles in life was the feeling of low self-worth when it came to my oldest son. Little did I know how true God was to His Word when He says that all things are working for our good. For the longest time, I never wanted my son to get a cellular phone. It wasn't that I wanted to be mean or unfair, but I wanted to protect him from outside influences as much as possible. I knew that once he got a cellular phone of his own, it would diminish my control over his outside influences. I felt like my husband's decision to get him the phone one

Christmas was the biggest mistake he could have made. But what I didn't realize was that even though he didn't talk much with his mouth, he texted a whole lot.

So even if I only had to ask a simple question or just wanted to see how his day was going, I would text instead of calling. I seemed to get more out of him this way. It became a means of communication not only for him to ask for things he didn't want to ask us in person, but also a means for him to let me know that he left his lunch at home and he didn't get to eat that day, or even more so, that he ate lunch, but that it was nasty and that all frozen dinners aren't as great as they look on the box. Even if we were in the same house, it became a means of communication for us to talk secretly about Father's Day gifts and birthday gifts for my husband. We made a game out of it. The more I texted him, the more he texted back, oftentimes about nothing significant. If it was nothing more than a smiley face emoticon or link to a video, we began to communicate better than we ever had in the past. God had used the very thing that I was afraid of, fearful of, and downright against, to work in my favor. As my pastor always says, in this iPod generation, we cannot reach people with an eight-track ministry. So whereas families used to sit down and play board games, or watch favorite sitcoms together, that wouldn't get too many positive results in my house.

It was through a youth retreat that God gave me something to share with him that no one else had shared yet. I wasn't there for his natural birth. I wasn't there for his first steps and his first words. I didn't get the experience of watching his first tooth fall out and grow back. But God had given me something almost more important than all of those things. It was Memorial Day weekend, and it was time for my church's annual youth retreat, which took place at a campground site in upper Michigan, secluded and away from busy civilization. Because I was a part of the youth ministry staff, I had been to the past few retreats. But this was the first retreat that my son was able to attend. He didn't know what to expect, but I did.

Most of our youth who attended these retreats were changed forever. They didn't come back on the bus the same way they went to the campsite. Something miraculous happened for those who came to the retreat seeking and expecting something great from God. They came back with a stronger relationship with Christ. They came back with a greater consciousness of their actions and decisions. They made promises to God, even in their youth, to keep His Word and commandments. So I didn't know exactly what God was going to do in my son's life, but I knew that when he came back, he would be different in some way.

It was during this weekend that my son received the Holy Ghost with the evidence of speaking in other tongues. His father wasn't there. His biological mother had passed on. But I was there. Even though my husband and I were married at the time that he was baptized, I somehow managed to miss that day too. Although I had missed many monumental moments in his life, including his water baptism, I was there for the spiritual baptism. There was a time in my life where I thought I would never be filled with the Holy Ghost because I was baptized and it hadn't happened for so many years. So I was ecstatic that my son had not only been baptized, but filled with the Holy Ghost all by the age of 14. I knew that he was still a teenager and would make mistakes. He still had many life challenges yet to conquer. But God was not only with him, but in him, every step of the way from that day forth.

I wanted to tell the world about his celebration! I posted it on Twitter and Facebook, and I texted over fifty people in my phone. It was as if a new baby had just been born and I had to tell everybody. I was so proud of him for opening up to God and allowing Him to have His way in his life that weekend. Just from my experience of attending these retreats in the past, it took way more for our young men to open up to God than it did for the young ladies. We often found the young ladies crying out to God, lying out on the floor, hollering and screaming, seeking the Lord for something greater than they had obtained before. The young men were usually cool and calm, until the spirit of the Lord did something extraordinary in the place, causing them all to end up in a corner crying out or laying before God at the altar. But this particular day, because of the number of youth at the altar and laid out throughout the place, numerous youth were taken into a private hallway to pray for the evidence of speaking tongues. While I was on stage with the praise team and was not able to be there face to face with my son when he received it, I was elated that he had received it there and I was the only family member there to share that experience with him. It probably didn't mean anything to him at the time. Maybe it will hold greater weight to him later in life. But for me, it meant the world. It meant new life for him and for me.

Though his actions at home didn't change much, and while he still remained a pretty reserved person, something in his worship changed whenever he got into the presence of the Lord at church. He was more apt to raise his hands, to close his eyes, to talk to God in his own way. In our youth services, we tend to have a lot of spectators, and unfortunately not enough participators. But he began to set the standard and example for the other youth who are usually afraid or 'too cool' to open up totally to God. Not only did he set the example for other youth, but in troubling times, he often set the example for me.

I remember a time when it seemed like my marriage was over. Both my husband and I had made the decision that it was time for a divorce. We sat the kids down and explained to them both what we had decided and who would be living with whom. My son, who was now 14, would often ask in his early age of about 7 when we first married, if his father and I ever divorced where he would live and where his little brother would live. But his response this time was entirely different. When we asked him who he would like to live with his response was that it didn't really matter to him. This surprised me for two reasons. In my own immature thinking, I guess I always assumed if we ever did split, that since he came into the marriage with his father, he would leave with his father. I also assumed that he simply viewed me as a stepparent, not his 'real' mother, almost just as a person who was filling in for the time being for someone else who couldn't fulfill her duties. But again, he proved me to have underestimated him.

Later on that particular day, I remember going to speak to him in private where just he and I could talk. He didn't seem worried. He didn't seem stressed at all by our recent decision. This not only worried me, but scared me that he would somehow grow up holding his feelings in instead of letting them out. But when I asked him a question about how he felt about our decision, he simply said, "It hasn't happened yet." This was a very mature way of looking at the situation. Here we were as two adults, going through emotional changes and making emotional decisions, yet my son seemed unaffected. I didn't think much of his comment then, but over time, it began to minister to me in its own way. So many times, even as faithful Christians, we worry about things that have not yet happened. We begin to confess our demise before the walls come tumbling down. We begin to profess our defeat before the first sight of trouble even arises, even if it is contradictory to the Word of God we claim to believe.

But my son genuinely wasn't worried. As far as he could see, as long as we all were still in the same house, there was still time for prayer and he knew enough about God to know that prayer does change things. I asked him to genuinely keep the family in prayer, and I believe that he did just that. Through it all, he remained cool. He was calm. We never saw him break down emotionally. He never asked us again if we changed our minds or if we were still going to go through with it or not. He simply watched and waited. Needless to say, my husband and I never divorced. But we were more worried than my son ever was. Maybe he had greater faith in God than we did at the time, but his simple philosophy of "It hasn't happened yet" may have saved the family from total dismemberment.

The same attitude should be taken when we encounter daily challenges and life's struggles. While some may be bigger than others, we often run and hide at the mere thought of trouble coming our way. We go to the doctor and they say that they see a mass or tumor, and we automatically assume it is cancer. There hasn't been an official diagnosis yet, but we have already planned our demise before the doctor can even finish running proper tests. Our mortgages fluctuate to dollar amounts we financially cannot afford to pay. But before we even get a foreclosure notice, we are already fearful of being homeless, out on the streets, with no roof over our head. We go into work one day and hear rumors of cuts on the job and layoffs to come. Our boss has not pulled us into an office yet and no one has told us to box up our belongings from our desk. Yet we have already begun to worry about how we will make it, how we will pay our bills, how long it will take us to find another job and where our next meal will come from. But the one factor we always seem to dismiss in the midst of worrying is that *it hasn't happened yet!*

You can drive yourself crazy worrying about the 'what ifs' of life. All the while, God is saying to us, "But it hasn't even happened yet. I still have time to turn it around." Where the problem comes in is when we don't see the way out, we begin to not only waver in our faith, but ultimately lose it until God gets tired of our moaning and complaining like big crybabies and rescues us from what seemed like a huge problem, but really wasn't a problem to Him at all. Sure, the doctor may see something on an X-ray, but it hasn't been confirmed to be cancer. Yes, the mortgage has adjusted much more than your income has adjusted, but as long as you have a roof over your head, you can't worry about *possible* foreclosure. And often the rumors of pink slips floating around the office are just that, rumors! Even if they are true, who's to say that this time, they won't pass over you with the pink slips and instead give it to your coworker who sits across from you? Until it *happens*, these are all just scare tactics the enemy uses to get us off focus from what we should be doing for the Kingdom of God. He wants to scare us out of operating in our God-given purpose and destiny. He wants to confuse us about who we are and most importantly, *whose* we are. If he can get you to doubt God, because your situation at the time seems so much bigger than the power of God, he can send you into a world spiraling out of control where you fall into a spiritual rut and can't seem to ever get out.

In essence, this is what I was doing. I stayed on my face and attended many prayer meetings, praying that God would turn the situation around. But in the back of my mind, for a season, I didn't really believe that it was in His will *to* turn it around. Yet, the simple but profound philosophy my son had deposited into me kept ringing in my head. *It hasn't happened yet.* Isaiah 11:6 says ...*and a little child will lead them.* Though he wasn't very little in stature, he was still considered a child legally. He probably didn't know the depth of what he spoke, but I was glad that God used him in a mighty way, even in his youth. He knew we attended church regularly, and he knew we believed in the power of prayer. Yet, during this season, he didn't see us put much of it into action. It was time for us to practice that which we claimed to believe so faithfully, not just for us, but because he, of all people, was definitely watching.

Residue of his spiritual rebirth was becoming more and more evident in the little things he said or did. It didn't come in a loud shout or a quick sprint around the church. He was still a very reserved and quiet person. But when he did speak, he spoke profoundly and ministered in a simple way, probably not even knowing the impact of what he was saying. His day of rebirth had not only transformed him, but it transformed me. Salvation and dedication to Christ is often a selfish thing. Nobody can do it for you and no one can make you do it or stick to it. It has to be a personal desire for God and the things of God and nothing of the outside world. But even though this was between him and God, I was on the sideline taking notes. In a moment's time, the child became the teacher, and I had to respect the authority of the words God had placed in him. So even in your present storms or what seems to be impossible situations, remember the simple words of my son: *It hasn't happened yet.*

Tenita C. Johnson

The Prayer of the Heart

It always amazes me how God hears our prayers, even the ones that are not necessarily spoken out loud. But it's great to know that He hears the heart and its desires, even more so than we do sometimes. It is also amazing to know that whatever Word God has spoken into your life, it will not return void. It will set out to accomplish that which He intended it to do. Sometimes, God can speak so many words over our lives that we become overwhelmed and get ahead of God, or we forget what has been spoken, not because it's not important to us, but because so much has been spoken over a period of time.

Recall that I lost a set of twins, one of which was a baby girl. At the time, I didn't think it mattered to me whether it was a boy or a girl; I just wanted healthy babies. But I lost them both. I then gave birth to a baby boy a year later after the loss. Though this was my first baby, this was my mother-in-law's fourth grandson, and she was petitioning heavily for a girl. To no avail, my sister-in-law also later gave birth to two boys. But at a point in my life when I hadn't yet even given birth to any of my children, it was spoken to me that I would be the one to bear the only girl grandchild. I didn't think anything of the word at the time. People spoke things over me all the time; some came to pass and some didn't. But every time I got pregnant, this prophetic word rang in my ears, hopeful. Even in the midst of numerous miscarriages, I always wondered, *Was that the girl?*

When I was a little girl, I always said that I would have four kids. After all, I was the only child and was always bored and lonely, and I didn't want my kids to experience that. So in the back of my mind, though I had my stepson and had given birth to another baby boy, I still had two more kids to go to reach my goal. My two boys were far apart in age, so I definitely felt the need to have more. It was almost a challenge of fulfillment. Not only was my challenge to have more children, but to give my husband a girl. Though he acted like he didn't care to have a girl at all, and we always joked about the many fears he had of having to raise a girl, I think deep down he wanted one too.

My son, Xavier Zachariah, was born in August 2004. But when I became pregnant seven years later in 2011, I was sure it was another boy. After all, we hadn't had a girl all this time. Why would God give us a girl now? It was around Thanksgiving of that year that I found out that I indeed was pregnant with a girl! It seemed unreal. I kept asking for ultrasounds to make sure they didn't see anything between the legs (indicating that it was a boy instead). I even asked the ultrasound technician how certain she was and if she had ever been wrong at determining the sex of the baby. She had been doing this for over fifteen years, so I guess I had to trust her judgment. It was finally a girl. The word that had been spoken to me long before my son was born in 2004 had not come to fruition until the fall of 2011, almost eight or nine years later. But even with the beginning of the manifestation of a promise, fear and doubt crept in.

I worried about losing her, even though I was well into my fourth month. I knew from prior pregnancies that I was considered high risk and the doctors even took extra precaution to stop me from going into pre-term labor. I still had thoughts of loss. I feared losing her while she was in the womb. I feared dying myself during childbirth. On May 5, 2012, I gave birth to a healthy baby girl—Nyla Janae. But, even after she was here, I still feared losing her. Her first few days at home, she slept a lot and lost weight, which sent me into even greater fear, even though I knew it was normal for newborns to lose some weight the first week. The enemy had put his tactics into full attack, even in the midst of our celebrating the arrival of our new baby girl.

But then there was a part of me that remembered what God had promised me. I had not prayed for a baby girl out loud, per se. But I guess God knew what was planted deeply in my heart. He knew my innermost desire. I wasn't sure I even understood my extreme desire or why it was so important to me, but deep down, it was. I'm glad that God knows the desires of our heart, and when we are faithful to Him, it is His pleasure to grant us those desires. Though it was years later, and I may have had forgotten about the promise that was spoken, God did not. His word had come to pass. God had not only fulfilled his word, but He had also restored that which was lost. I knew for a fact that I had lost a girl when I lost the twins. Though I wondered what the sex of the babies were when I went through numerous miscarriages, I like to believe that God was restoring the lost when He gave me Nyla.

What the enemy ultimately tried to use as a weapon against my mind and my spirit, God eventually turned it around and used it to work for my good. Had I not lost multiple babies, maybe I would not have been as grateful for my kids being born healthy and normal. Though I had not specifically asked God to restore, He had done just that. That's the thing I love about God. He may not come when we call out to Him. He may not restore things that we have lost along the way, right away. But rest assured, God has not forgotten what He has promised you or what you have prayed for in your secret closet. If it doesn't happen today, it can happen tomorrow. If it doesn't happen tomorrow, it can happen next week. If not next week, next month. But it *will* happen. Our timing is not God's timing, and I know from experience that He does things in His own timing, not necessarily when we want Him to move.

I challenge you to do the hardest thing that most of us just flat out don't want to do—wait! Though I lost a baby boy and baby girl in 2003, I gained a baby boy back in 2004 and a baby girl back in 2012. God doesn't give you an expected date of arrival when He promises something. He just speaks, and it's up to you to praise while you wait and look for the manifestation, without murmuring and complaining about the waiting process. Don't despise every storm and don't curse every crisis. We endure the majority of the things we go through for two reasons: to make us stronger and to be a living testimony for someone who will go through something similar in the future. Although we can't see the benefits of a storm while we are in it, know that it, too, is working for your good and that when you come out on the other side, you will be a better *you*. Not only will you look back and wonder how you made it through, but you will learn the purpose of a storm as you grow in Christ and mature in His Word.

The saying, "What doesn't kill you will only make you stronger" is not just a phrase to recite to people when they are going through. Those words are true to no end when it comes to the Word and the promises of God. Every trap the enemy sets is formed to destroy you. If he can't kill you physically, he'll kill you financially. If he can't kill you financially, he'll kill you mentally. The enemy is very strategic in his plans, and he is not necessarily going to just take you out with a bullet or tragic accident. The Bible talks about the enemy desiring to sift us as wheat. When I watch my husband sift flour and sugar for his cakes, he sifts more than once. I'm always fascinated by the large crystals of sugar that are left in the sifter that were too big to fall through with the rest of the sugar, but small enough that we wouldn't notice it with a human eye if we were simply pouring the sugar into our cup of coffee. He repeats the process about three or four times before he finally pours his sugar or flour into a bowl to make his cake batter. The same is true of the enemy. He attempts to sift us daily and sometimes, God allows him to. He does it little by little. It may start with something as simple as someone cutting you off while driving on the highway. When you get to work, a co-worker wastes coffee on your new shoes. Then an angry customer curses you out on the telephone. Before you know it, your whole day is destroyed and you have given in to the sifting process, without even knowing it. Now for some people, this is not enough to get them to take their focus off of God and the purpose that He has for their life. But for others, this could send them into a world of trouble, filled with drinking, drugs and ultimately leaving the church, giving up on life in general because they feel they just can't catch a break.

Everything has a purpose. We don't go through things just to be 'going through'. Just as the enemy is very strategic in his tactics and goals, so is God when it comes to the tests and purpose He has for each test He allows to hit our doorstep. Nothing just happens. But for every fire God has taken you through, and will take you through in the future, know that He is burning off things you don't need in the next season, things that may hinder you from where you are going or even more so, people holding you back from your God-given destiny. Nobody promised that the process of purification would be easy or that you would only need to be purified once. We die to ourselves daily, so there will be multiple fires before we are purified and come out as pure gold. But one thing is for certain—you will come out as pure gold when it's all said and done!

Intentionally Specific

In the summer of 2011, during a rough and troubling time in my life, God laid it on my heart to start listing my prayers out on paper. Not only did I begin to do this, but I didn't do it alone. My cousin, who was miles away in West Virginia, graciously kept the list for me to remind me what we had already seen come to pass and what was yet to come and needed to remain on the list. Had I known to do this a long time ago, I may have received more positive results in my prayer requests. But God knows when to shift us into different methods of prayer. During this time of listing and praying, I strategically asked God to do some things in my marriage. Not only did He do everything on my list, but He exceeded my expectations and things my limited mind knew to ask for.

As the year progressed into the fall, I followed this same process with regard to my desired job. My cousin had asked me over the phone numerous times what my ideal job would be. So one day, she began to list them out for me on paper, just as we had done everything else. I specifically asked God for a job in my field of study, journalism, particularly in editing or proofreading. Not only did I want to edit, but I wanted to work in a marketing or advertising industry. I knew I wanted a full-time job. I wanted to be a hired-in employee; I had been contracting since I walked away from AT&T in 2007, and it was way too unstable. I also wanted full benefits, vacation time and sick time. But most of all, I wanted to work in a fun environment where I enjoyed going to work every day.

In December of 2011, I received a phone call for an interview, not knowing what it would lead to or what the company was all about. I nailed the interview, even after trying to hide my pregnancy by wearing a larger blazer in front of the hiring manager. I didn't want them to have any other reason to deny me the job, besides my not being qualified for the position. But I went in the door knowing that I was more than qualified for the position. A few days later, I received a call from the human resources department informing me that they wanted to make me an official offer of employment. I hadn't worked full-time since 2007. It was a long, long time coming, but God had heard my prayers.

At the time, I didn't remember everything I had listed on my prayer requests list with regard to a job. I knew the main thing was for me to be hired in full-time. But when I called my cousin to let her know about the job, she began to run down the list and check everything off that I had asked for. It was a full-time position. I was not a contractor, but an actual employee of the company. Not only did I have full medical, dental and vision benefits, but I also had sick time and vacation time. It was a position as an editor with a marketing and advertising firm. I had been very specific about my prayers, and God had been very specific when He answered them. But the thing I love about God is that He always exceeds our miniscule prayer requests. He manages to go above and beyond, just because of who He is.

This was not only a job, but a place where I could make a long-term career. In addition to the wonderful benefits package, the company provided free parking to all of its employees. They often ordered food for the team when we had to stay in the office and work later than normal. From time to time, they barbecued on the third-floor patio and provided lunch for the whole company. Coffee and hot chocolate were complimentary every day, all day. They even had an old-fashioned popcorn machine where you could pop it fresh right there in the lobby of the building. And although I was a salaried employee, I was eligible for overtime pay after any hours over 40 per week. This was a big deal for me since I had only heard of hourly employees being paid overtime, while salaried workers usually work a minimum of 40 hours but work way more without additional pay. It was a very fun, creative atmosphere. I often heard my friends complain about going to work day in and day out, but this was a place where I didn't mind going every day. Not only did I like the work, but I liked the people and work environment as a whole. That is something I could not have paid for. But to have peace when you go to work every day is worth millions to the mind.

The thing about God is that He doesn't always move when we want Him to. There are some things He has to take us through to purify us in Him even further. Through the process, we come out knowing Him better, trusting Him more and having a greater testimony to tell the next person we encounter who may be going through the same thing. But it's going to happen in His timing, not ours. He knows just what we need when we need it. Had God given me this job immediately after I walked away from that position in 2007, I wouldn't know how great a provider He is to His children. In a matter of almost five years of unemployment, and contract jobs here and there, I never missed a meal. I was never set out on the streets. I never received a shut-off notice. All of my bills somehow, some way remained paid in full and good standing. That's nothing but the hand of God that sustained us in what could have been a season of stress and worry.

We know that God is a God of excellence, but He is also a God of specifics. Even though He already knows our heart, our wants, and our desires, He still requires us to ask for some things. When we ask, we need to be certain we not only know what we are asking for, but the consequences, good or bad, when we ask. People may ask God to make them a better steward over their money, but they aren't willing to pay tithes and offering, so He has to put them in a place where they wish they could just pay tithes and offering because they are struggling so much financially. Some people ask God for bigger houses and cars, but then they lose them because they weren't prepared to pay the note on time or cover the financial costs for routine maintenance. As believers, many of us ask God for greater anointing. Realize, though, that with greater anointing may come greater devils on your back. It may bring greater trials so that God can truly put your faith to the test.

It may require you losing your job and everything you own for God to show you Who the true provider of your every need is. Many people think of their job as their source and when the company shuts down or starts passing out pink slips, people lose their minds. Some commit suicide. Some start robbing banks or gas stations to make ends meet instead of depending on God. But how soon we forget that not too long before all of these tragic things happening in our lives, we asked God for greater anointing. You really have to ask yourself, "Do I really know what I am praying for?"

When the Smoke Clears: A Phoenix Rises

Not only do you need to be intentionally specific in your prayers, but you also need to pray specifically according to God's will for your life. It may not be His will for you to have a Bentley right now; you may have to drive a Honda first. He may not give you the house on a hill in a wealthy suburb with maids and servants just yet if He knows you won't appreciate it. We have our set agendas for our lives, but we must also be willing to yield to the will of God. According to His Word, you already know that He is not out to hurt or harm you in His will. You know that He wants us to prosper in all things. So even if you feel like you have a great plan and you really want some things to happen in that plan, be open to a slight detour or change of service, if you will, should God decide that He has something better in store.

Tenita C. Johnson

When the Smoke Clears

Many are familiar with the popular bible story of the three Hebrew boys who were thrown into a fiery furnace. King Nebuchadnezzar told everyone in Babylon that when they heard any type of music, they had to bow down and worship the golden image he crafted. Well, everyone did—except Shadrach, Meshach and Abednego. They knew that it was not the true and living God they served, so they took a stand and chose not to bow down, regardless of what those around them were doing. So you know what that meant; into the fire they went. But before they were even placed in the fire, they politely told the king that the God they served was more than well able to deliver them from the fiery furnace. Even if He didn't, they still made it clear that they would not serve or worship the god that the king set up.

I imagine that people around them watching were silently begging and pleading with them to just bow down and get it over with. After all, bowing down to a false image couldn't be nearly as bad as being burned in a fire that, by the way, was turned up seven times hotter than it usually was. I'm not sure why the king had the three men bound before they were thrown into the fire. It's not like once you were in the furnace, you could simply climb out and not take a certain measure of flames with you and yet still be on fire, even if you did make it out. But maybe the king was naïve enough to believe that there was a possibility that they could escape.

But isn't that just like the enemy? He wants to not only keep us under attack, in the fire, and forever going through rough times, but he wants to keep us bound. I see the three Hebrew boys being bound as a spiritual sign more so than a natural sign. So many times in life, people are delivered and set free from struggles and strongholds, but their minds are still bound. Their finances are still bound. Their relationships even suffer from the baggage and residue and become bound. The Word of God, however, tells us that He comes to set the captive free, and that he whom He sets free, is free indeed.

So, to King Nebuchadnezzar's surprise, not only were the three Hebrew boys walking around in the fire, un-scorched and unburned, but they were no longer bound. They were walking around in the fire freely. Not only were they walking around in the fire, free and unbound, but there was a fourth party who had joined them in the fire. They weren't screaming and hollering for help. They weren't even running around trying to get out. Maybe the Holy Ghost got into the fire with them and spoke to them ever so softly to tell them not to freak out, not to scream, cry or holler, but to simply trust Him and take a walk in the midst of the fire. Because they were secure in who He was and knew His track record, they probably received these instructions well, put their total trust in Him and began to move into place.

There's a lot to be taken from the story of the three Hebrew boys in the fiery furnace, and pastors worldwide have put their own spin on teaching it so that congregations get a different meaning and takeaway every time. These boys displayed extreme faith in God and were willing to take the pain and agony of being burned to prove that they trusted only in the *true* and *living* God. I don't recall their ever complaining before they were thrown into the fire. I don't even think they begged the person throwing them in to have mercy and pity and reconsider. Something within them told them that no matter what was going on inside that furnace, God would not let them down and everything would be alright.

Some, if not most of us, have been in spiritual fires before. Everything around us is going crazy. Bills are past due. Children are acting out in school and at home. Your car is on its last leg. Your husband just asked for a divorce. Your job is giving out pink slips for Christmas instead of holiday bonuses. To top it all off, you've just been diagnosed with a terminal illness. This would be our definition, in the modern world, of being put in the fiery furnace and it being turned up seven times hotter. We consider a pink slip from the job bad, and that may be a small fire. When the brakes on the car go out, we consider that an even bigger fire, especially if we don't have the money to get the repairs done at that moment. Now we begin to worry how we will get back and forth to work, who will take the kids to school and how much gas money they will want for doing all of it because most "friends" won't drive you and yours around the city for free.

These are small fires to us. But when everything begins to hit the fan at once, we do one of two things. We either murmur and complain and adopt the victim mentality, or we cling closer to God, pray more, fast more, tithe more, and adopt the victor mentality. The choice ultimately is yours. With God, faith in Him and perception can mean everything and determine how long your fire lasts. I would implore you to adopt the latter. Complaining doesn't add one blessing to your life, and it doesn't make God move any faster. All that tells Him is that there are still some things that need to be worked out, purified and pressed out through this trying process. Thus, He leaves you in the fire a little longer. But I believe that when we change our perceptions and perspectives of the situation, God can meet us right where we are, show us what we need to see, and bring us out victoriously.

Not only does murmuring and complaining tell God that there are some things that still need to be drawn out of you, but it also tells Him that in the rougher times, you truly don't trust Him to bring you out. It's easy to say, "God, I trust you" when the bills are paid, the car is brand new off the lot and your home resembles that of *The Brady Bunch*; but what do you do when you have numerous shut-off notices sitting on your dining room table? What do you do when your car is twenty years old, the transmission just went out, and you don't have a way to get the kids to school or for you to make it to work? Everything is a test of faith. The enemy's full-time, hired-in position is to get you to curse God, to give up on God, to seek other ways to pay your bills instead of waiting on God to make a way out of *what seems* like no way.

Anybody in his or her right mind knows that fire is hot. It's not comfortable, and it's not meant to be a permanent situation. Some people are in the fire because God needs to burn off their bad attitude. Some are in the fire because God needs to get that person to trust Him more. He wants to prove to them that He is the ultimate provider, Jehovah Jireh. Others are in the fire out of pure disobedience. I like to refer to myself as Jonah a lot. God may not put me in the fire, but he may put me in a holding place until I do what I know He has told me to do. Some people have outright disobeyed God, and they wonder why they are catching so much hell on earth. It's simply because you know God told you *not* to do something, and you did it anyway, or vice versa.

My mother, my cousins, even some of my close friends will tell you I am what parents call hard-headed. I am a person who has to learn for myself and sometimes, that means learning the hard way. That's not the case all the time, but most times it is. As believers, sometimes we are just downright hard-headed. You know God told you not to take that job, but you wanted the money and didn't see how God would make a way otherwise, so you took it anyway. Now you can't stand going to work. You hate your boss and you feel like the whole team is against you. Yet, you want God to deliver you from this fiery furnace of a job. I even have a friend who has told me directly that in her first marriage, she clearly heard the Lord speak to her at the altar telling her that she should not marry the man she was standing before! But because she was looking in the natural, wondering what people would think, what they would say, she said, "I do" anyhow. Of course it ended in divorce because God told her in the first place that he was not her husband and that she should not marry him. But women in particular, once we've bought our thousand-dollar wedding gown, picked out bridesmaids dresses, groomed our children to be a flower girl and ring bearer, ten times out of ten, we are *not* cancelling our wedding. Unless the groom stands us up, we'll say, "I do" all the way to the altar, and be begging God in ten years to remove us, telling God, "I don't."

The purpose of the fire is not only to get you to trust God more and to have a greater relationship with Him, but to help you grow, both spiritually and naturally. I once heard a pastor say, "The purpose of the fire is to prepare me for what I can't handle right now—that which is on the way." Some of us are asking God for a Benz when we don't keep the Camry that He gave us clean and washed. We don't even want to pick people up for church in our new car. The sooner you learn that everything God gives to you isn't just for you, the better off you will be as a person. Taking it a step further, many women are praying for a husband, yet they don't dress nicely, they don't keep their hair done nicely, their kids are nasty and dirty and their home is a hot mess. No man in his right mind wants to walk into that and play Mr. Clean!

The bottom line is this—stay in the fire until God burns off everything that He needs to burn off to get you to your next level. It may be uncomfortable and you may not even understand the purpose of it right now, but stay in it. Even more so, while you're in it, don't murmur and complain and adopt the "Woe is me" mentality; praise God for the work He is doing and what is about to come. You won't be in the fire forever. God's not going to let you die in the fire. There are some things He needs to perfect in you that no one else can. If you would be real with yourself, you'd admit that *you* can't even change you! True change comes from God.

But when the fire is out, when the Lord has tried you and tested you according to His appointed time, you may smell like smoke, but you won't look like what you just came out of. You won't be burned. You won't be doused in soot. The old things will be left in the fire, in the ashes where God burned those things off of you. And although some people may know what you just came out of and may still see traces of smoke, when the smoke clears, you'll be all the better.

About Tenita C. Johnson

Too short and too dark, she never felt pretty. She referred to herself as ugly instead of waiting to hear it from someone else. Because no one told her that she mattered, she was worth the wait and she had great purpose, she found herself in numerous identity crises—searching for love in all the wrong places. For years, depression was Tenita Johnson's choice garment, until she made a conscious decision to shake off depression and put on the garment of praise.

Born to a fourteen-year-old mother, Tenita always felt like something was missing. Despite baptism as a child and regular church attendance with her grandmother, it wasn't until adulthood that she realized God was the missing piece. She knew the God of her matriarchs, but she had to know Him for herself.

From losing a set of twins the day after her wedding to years of unemployment, suicidal thoughts and blended family woes, she learned that the only way out of the fire was to go through it. Every fire was orchestrated by God to burn some things off of her to make her better. Every fire gave her a testimony to encourage others. Overcoming depression positioned her to pull others out of darkness. Experiencing miscarriages set her up to minister to women with barren wombs. Unemployment taught her to embrace Philippians 4:19.

The young girl who thought she wasn't good enough blossomed into a woman who knows that she is more than enough. She makes a deliberate choice to live her best life and walk in her God-given purpose. She encourages others that a predetermined victory follows every test.

About So It Is Written

Tenita C. Johnson's vast knowledge of writing styles and keen eye for spelling and grammatical errors, allows her to transform others' thoughts and ideas into written masterpieces.

Through So It Is Written, she is committed to perfecting manuscripts for successful publishing. She coaches authors—novice or expert—to bury boring bios. Her press releases have drawn attention from media thus creating distinct brand images long before the books hit the shelves.

With a bachelor's degree in journalism and two decades of industry experience, she seeks to form relationships, not build a database of clientele.

SoItIsWritten.net
info@soitiswritten.net

When the Smoke Clears: A Phoenix Rises

100 Words of Encouragement: Tidbits of Inspiration
By Tenita C. Johnson

Who's in the Driver's Seat?

You don't need a global positioning system (GPS) with God as your guide. With Him in the driver's seat, you are always headed in the right direction—His will. He knows your beginning and ending and He's the best one to lead you to the desired end. So take your hands off the steering wheel, slide over to the passenger seat and let Him drive. He'll get you there safe and on time!

"A must-have in your life."
—Kim Brooks, author of *He's Fine, But is He Saved?*

"*100 Words of Encouragement* is for those who want to stay encouraged, motivated and inspired to live the abundant life that God came to give."
—First Lady Crisette Ellis, Greater Grace Temple-Detroit

ISBN-13: 978-0-9825984-0-5
Retail price: $9.95 US

Available at **SoItIsWritten.net** and Amazon.com

Stones of Inspiration Blog

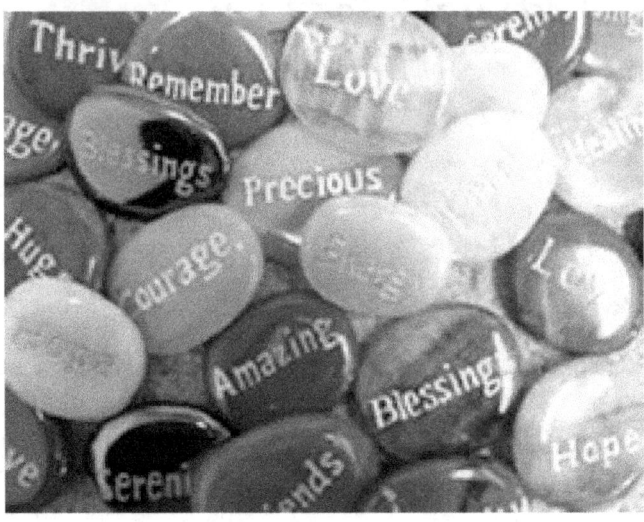

Stones of Inspiration was birthed through the encouragement of small, yet profound pocket stones. Although each stone may only contain one word, that word has the power to transform one's day, one's life, one's mind. Whether the stones speak to hope or love, it can be a small whisper to one person or a loud scream to another. Nonetheless, this blog seeks to bring small moments of hope, faith and encouragement that have the power to make a big difference in your day.

StonesOfInspiration.wordpress.com

When the Smoke Clears: A Phoenix Rises

For speaking engagements or to order additional copies of
When the Smoke Clears

Tenita C. Johnson
313.999.6942
SoItIsWritten.net
info@soitiswritten.net

* * * * * * * * * * * * * * * * * *

Please mail _____ copies of

When the Smoke Clears

_____
Name
_____
Address
_____
City / State / Zip
(_____)_____
Phone
_____
Email

Quantity	Price Per Book	Total
	$12.95	
Sales Tax (MI residents add $0.78 or 6% per book)		
Shipping ($3.49 first book, $0.99 each additional)		
Grand Total* (Payable to: So It Is Written)		

* Certified check and money orders only

Also Available on Amazon.com

www.ingramcontent.com/pod-product-compliance
Lightning Source LLC
Chambersburg PA
CBHW072055290426
44110CB00014B/1692